T0365369

TEN
GENERATIONS

A Family History

Written by David More

Trafford
PUBLISHING®

 www.trafford.com

North America & international
toll-free: 1 888 232 4444 (USA & Canada)
fax: 812 355 4082

Contents

Acknowledgements

I am truly grateful to Jean Cruickshank for this opportunity. She not only attended my local history course at St. Lawrence College in Kingston, and bought my books, but then contacted me to see if I might be interested in putting together her family's story. It has been a wonderful journey through time. I am happy and proud to have been commissioned to create this little book about her extraordinary family.

Except where indicated, all illustrations are from family archives.

Introduction

Research into family trees is fraught with peril, and the farther back one goes, the more perilous it necessarily becomes, because the increase in distance from the present viewer not only shrinks the quantity and quality of written records dramatically, and as is the case of some families described here, eventually descends entirely into legend, but also dramatically increases the number of recorded inaccuracies and mistakes. For instance, Rose Hill, Edinburgh, is also referred to as Rosedale, in one well-researched family tree. Similarly, Frederick George Heriot is often confounded with his brother George Heriot, who was Deputy Postmaster General, a mistake recorded in the Dictionnaire Larousse of 1885. Modern research tools and the vast, ever growing body of digitized archival material available on the web have revealed many common mistakes perpetuated by supposed authorities, sometimes over hundreds of years.

This amazing family story deserves to be told, and perhaps future generations will be able pick up the torch and follow some of the intriguing leads farther than was possible in the scope of this book. Certainly, there are dozens more accounts and more distant family branches to follow up. Names like de Belin, Johnson, Heriot, Nugent, Campbell, Sheppard, De Lancey, Watkins, Newton and many others have illustrious histories of their own, but these necessarily have to be left for others to discover and unravel.

It is a wonderfully challenging experience to read 19th century handwritten letters, which were written in one direction and then crosswise over top of the original to save paper and postage costs! Image selection was difficult, there are many more to choose from, but I did attempt, with the family's assistance, to use those that evoked the people and the times the best.

I take full responsibility for the accuracy of this book, and any errors that I have perpetuated or created are not intended to create new legends. No need to – this exceptionally interesting family has participated in many of the significant events of the English, Scottish, French and Dutch-speaking world since the middle 1500s.

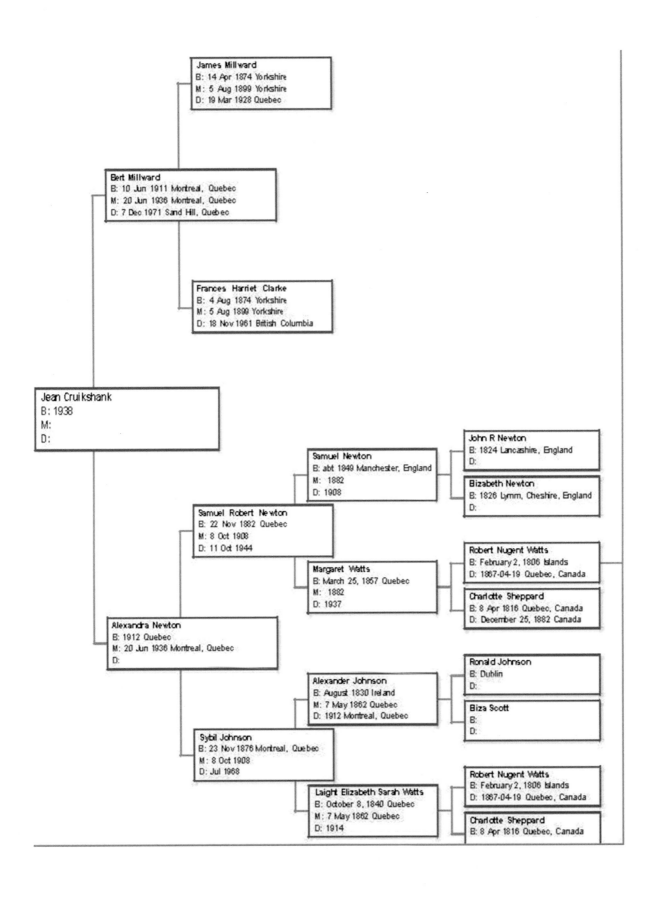

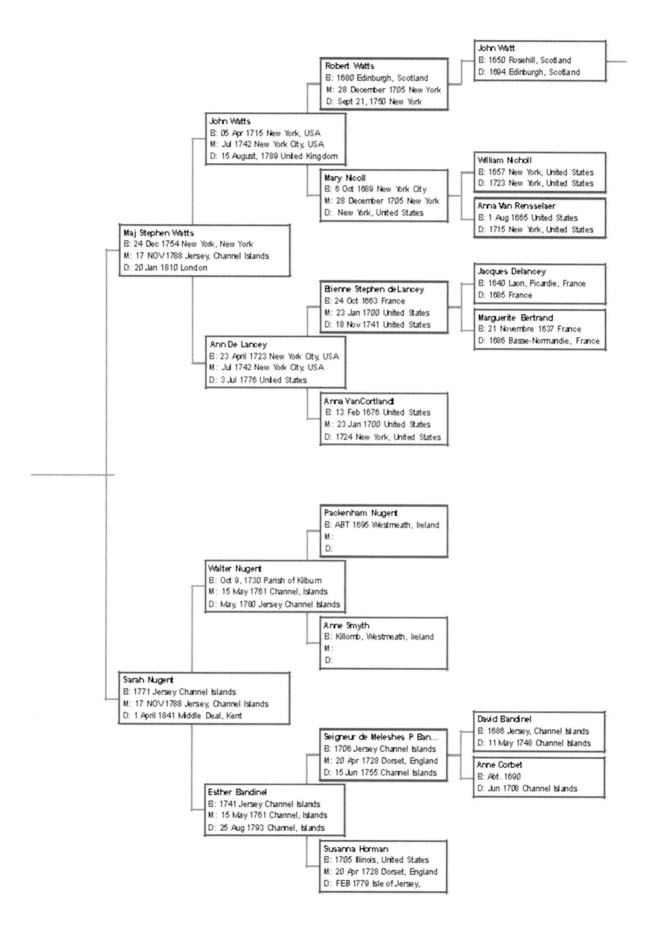

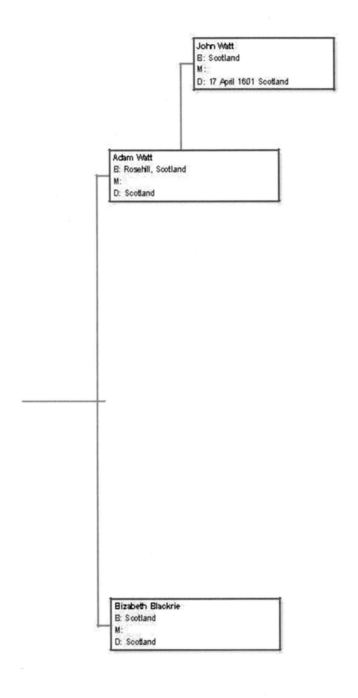

John Watt
B: Scotland
M:
D: 17 April 1601 Scotland

Adam Watt
B: Rosehill, Scotland
M:
D: Scotland

Bizabeth Blackrie
B: Scotland
M:
D: Scotland

Beginnings

Three Generations of the Watt family in Edinburgh

(1596—1700)

John Watt, Deacon of the Trades and well-known Edinburgh mason, was shot to death on the Burgh-moor in September of 1601. He was not of the royal blood, but his murder alarmed James VI, the King of Scotland. Were the Presbyterians in revolt once more? The process of assigning guilt was critically important to him. Investigations into the deaths of commoners, even important, wealthy and influential commoners, are not something Kings normally take much interest in. But ticklish negotiations were underway. Elizabeth I was dying and James Stuart was quietly working to ensure that he would assume the throne of England upon her death. No, the thing had better be done right, or there might be serious repercussions.

Not to say the King wasn't grateful to the man, for John Watt had, after all, saved his life five years before in the coup attempt that had driven the Royal Court right out of Edinburgh for several months. Watt was well hated for that loyalty by important people, including Robert Bruce, the Moderator of the Scottish Church, who had called down a heavenly judgment against him. As one historian noted, "Such . . . prognostications of judgments are of course very likely to bring their own fulfillment."

This curse was most likely a retaliation for Watt's own threat to "*invade the person of the Minister*" which had endeared Watt to his King, although not to Bruce, the pious man of the cloth. But James VI was, above all, a practical and ambitious ruler, whose lust for England's crown began when he was young; long before Elizabeth executed his mother, Mary, Queen of Scots, for treason. It was in his interest to discover who murdered John Watt. Or not.

Truly, there were important and delicate issues of state involved in who might be convicted of the crime, and how the proceedings were conducted. A false conviction could have very significant political consequences. The king was accordingly "exact" with regard to the trial of the chief suspect, who was found innocent. No other perpetrator was ever prosecuted.[1]

John Watt is one of the earliest documented ancestors of Jean Cruickshank, and the Watt name dominates the family history for nearly 300 years. The mists of time continue to hide his birthdate. We know nothing of his parents, or his wife. Very often trades were passed from father to son. But it is likely that he was living in Edinburgh in 1553, working at his trade, or learning it, and thus would have heard the astounding roar of the largest gun in Edinburgh Castle – a siege bombard known as the "great iron murderer, *muckle-meg*" (Big Meg) — firing one of its gigantic, 300 pound stone balls two miles out onto Wardie Moor to celebrate the marriage of Mary, Queen of Scots, to France's François II.

Twenty years later, he also would have lived through the months-long cannonade by Elizabeth I's troops that reduced most of Edinburgh Castle to rubble during the *Lang Seige*. We know only a few things about the final five years of John Watt's life. We know he had at least one son, Adam. But certainly the mists of time on Scottish moors may well conceal links to a large and noble family established since the time of William the Conqueror in Yorkshire and Lancashire, some 200 miles to the south (see Appendix).

The 15[th,] and early 16th centuries in Britain were violent, no less so in Edinburgh. This was the era when the Wars of the Roses for the throne of England were followed by the tumult of the Tudor Reformation of the Catholic Church and then by the English Civil War between Royalists and Parliamentarians. Picking the wrong side in any of these events could, and did, divide and end many famous dynasties and lives. Scotland's fabric was also rent with its own civil wars between Catholics and the new Church of England.

Many other families perished in succeeding waves of plague, which killed 15% of the population in 1471 and perhaps another 20% in 1479-80. There were nine other general outbreaks of the Black Death in Britain between 1498 and 1665. Families fleeing these disasters scattered far and wide like dandelion seeds, and it is far from implausible that an offshoot of this northern English *Wattys* family, as they had come to be known by the time, should spring up in Edinburgh, or elsewhere.

But war, chaos and the growing power of the middle class also created opportunities that allowed individuals to rise out of social nowhere without necessarily having aristocratic family connections. If one had enough skill and perseverance to apprentice and become master of a skilled trade – no mean feat – one could achieve respect, especially if that valuable manual skill were accompanied by wit and daring and a bit of command presence – what we might now call leadership, or charisma.

This Scottish Watt family could also be the one which first appeared in written records a hundred years earlier in the late 15th Century, when one Martin Watt, mentioned as a "Chancellor of Glasgow" in 1496, had an official seal described in the Scottish College of Arms.[2] In the way that early records have of confounding researchers, Martin is not actually listed as one of the Chancellors in the records of the University of Glasgow, which was founded by Papal Bull a generation earlier, in 1451. At the time the Chancellors were all Catholic bishops, and Chancellor is not a term that relates to the town's government. So, who Martin was, why he had an official seal, and what he really did remains a mystery, as does his possible link to John Watt and his descendants.

But a century later the fog thins. John Watt first appears in 1596 as a representative for Edinburgh to the Scottish Parliament. He was certainly a leader. Not only had he become a Member of Parliament but he was also the Deacon of the Trades, or Crafts, in Edinburgh by that time. His occupation was listed as "mason" in the Roll of the Burgesses and Guild-Brethren of Edinburgh.

The political role probably followed from the others; masons were pre-eminent professionals linked by a very powerful and secretive guild at the time and they could certainly rise to literacy and wealth. Especially since they would have been in great demand to rebuild the shattered Castle. But John Watt's bravery and leadership had also earned the royal favour. He had personally saved James VI from an Edinburgh mob in riotous ferment about the King's proposed reforms of the Scottish Church. On December 17, 1596, John Watt had quickly organized and led a group of fellow tradesmen, who prevented the rioters from assaulting the King.

In his role as Deacon of the Trades, John Watt would almost certainly also have known George Heriot, the King's goldsmith, who lived about half a mile east of Edinburgh Castle. Heriot was a very famous Edinburgh family that, as we shall see, was to be linked forever by marriage to John Watt's North American descendants two centuries later on the Channel Islands.

In turbulent times, however, outspoken leadership and the King's favour are frequently double-edged swords. Later descendants of John Watt were to relearn this fact. His praiseworthy action supporting the young King and intemperate words against the senior Minister of the Scottish Church may well have resulted in his demise five years later. Robert Bruce was exiled for a time in 1596 for opposing royal policy, and religious schisms had ignited terrible, lingering passions. In any case, the murdered John Watt seems to have left behind a reasonably large estate, for Adam Watt, his son, appears next in the records of the time as a lawyer, following more war.

James VI succeeded Elizabeth Tudor in 1603 to become James I of England. He is perhaps best known for sponsoring a famous and lyrical translation of the Christian Bible. But he also held strong views about the supremacy of hereditary kings, and his son, Charles I, would carry these to an extreme that provoked revolution – the first revolution in the western world to succeed in breaking the absolute power of the monarchy. In particular, the issue of no taxation without parliamentary approval was contentious, and this would also figure prominently in the fate of later generations.

Charles I was executed for his treasonous actions by Oliver Cromwell in 1649, following a civil war between Parliamentarians and Royalists, and the republic known as the Commonwealth of England was established, which lasted until 1660. Thereafter, Kings and Queens of England have served at the pleasure of Parliament, not by divine right.

Three separate sieges of Edinburgh Castle occurred during struggles between the Crown and Scottish Covenanters, and between the Crown and Oliver Cromwell's Parliamentarians, before Adam Watt re-emerges from obscurity in 1661. Adam did not squander the advantage his father had gained in life. He was a well-educated man, which was not an asset easily come by. With it, he also possessed a canniness that enabled him to stickhandle his way successfully through decades of chaos and bloodshed.

Surviving the English civil war and the defeat and execution of Charles I and the years of Cromwell's Commonwealth, he continued his father's service to the Crown and was duly rewarded for it, for he appears in the records shortly after the restoration of Charles II to the throne of England, as a "Writer of the Signet". This was an important office, one of the eighteen Scottish solicitors entitled to the use of King's Signet to validate civil suit writs. He was also in charge of the Commissariat of Kircudbright district.

During that period Adam Watt lived at a place first mentioned in the available records at this time as Rose Hill, the pleasant memory of which would linger on in descendants who named farms after it in Manhattan. One 20th century family letter hints at a much more ancient provenance of the estate, the "family charter of John Watt of Rose Hill dates to 1124-1153 & of David, King of Scotland," but no other dependable trace of that ancestry has otherwise come to light.

Adam likely built the house at Rose Hill, which was still standing two hundred years later. If his father had constructed it before his death in 1601, its proximity to the Castle would most likely have doomed it during the wars and mayhem in and around Edinburgh. The house was built alongside the centuries-old Glasgow Road and had a sweeping view for miles downslope to the moors west of Edinburgh.

But less than half a mile to the east, the forbidding ramparts of Castle Rock, with Edinburgh Castle mounting high above it, loomed grimly over the estate like the former volcano it is. One can well imagine the frequent Edinburgh fogs swirling their dismal, clammy blankets about the place and shutting off the fine view.

Adam married, possibly a woman named Elizabeth Blackrie, and he named one of his sons, John, the other, Patrick. John was born around 1646, and he and his siblings were likely the first to be born in Rose Hill. John would grow up there, and so would his several children. One of those children, Robert Watt, was to establish the family in North America. Jean Cruickshank is one of Robert's descendants.

Nearly three centuries later, Rose Hill still stood — a substantial, old-fashioned, square building, plastered and painted yellow, mottled from the weather, 60 feet on a side. It was three stories high, with four evenly spaced windows on each floor, and a decorative belt of stone over the lowest windows, with a shallow-sloped, slate tile roof.

But in the 1880s no one bearing this Watt family name had lived in Edinburgh for nearly two centuries, and the house was doomed by the onrushing industrial age. Twenty years earlier, one Mr.

Burns, coal merchant, owned and lived in it and at that time it still had a "splendid" view to the west, with large grounds that were being leased, in part, to a market gardener — at least where the coal was not heaped up.

At the turn of the 19th century, the former Watt estate was almost entirely built over, and the Caledonian Railway's coal yard had expanded to squat where the house had been. If you visit the city today and walk along Gardner's Crescent, you are on what used to be Watt property.

There seems to be a bit of historical fog still drifting about Adam Watt's son John, but he is listed in one edition of Burke's Peerage as coming from Rose Hill, what was considered then a "small seat" near Edinburgh, and in another as a Lord of Session (lawyer in Scottish Court of Law). It is likely he was the Watt referred to as Commissioner of Supply for the County of Edinburgh in 1696, although one anonymous Ancestry.ca source has him dying in 1694 at Rose Hill. Doubtless even a small seat could provide income, and as a solicitor as well, he was likely fairly well off.

In any case, "small seat" or not, John's two sisters married well. Margaret married Sir Walter Riddell, Baronet, and Alice married another eminent man, Sir William Calderwood, Lord Polton. For Robert's aunts to marry into the minor nobility, the family must have been highly esteemed at the time in Edinburgh society. A grateful King may have awarded the Rose Hill estate to the original John, or to his son, Adam.

Robert Watt first gasped in and squalled lustily out the sweet Scottish air in 1680, in Rose Hill. He was one of the three sons of a mother who is not named in the records, as many were not, in those days of primogeniture and patriarchal rule. With his two brothers and two sisters they were the last generation of this Watt line in Scotland.

One of Robert's brothers, Adam, became an important man — Town Clerk of Edinburgh — and seems to have followed in his father's footsteps as Commissioner of Supply for the County of Edinburgh in 1704, dying in 1736. Adam also taught as a professor of Humanities in Edinburgh.

The other brother, John, immigrated to the colonies and was buried in Philadelphia in 1707. But both brothers died bachelors, and after Robert immigrated to the colonies, the Watt estate passed out of the hands of the family.

Generation Four

Robert Watts and Mary Nicoll

(1680-1750)

No Watt was ever to reclaim Rose Hill in Edinburgh, which remained standing until almost the beginning of the 20th century, but Watts were to flourish in North America. Robert's ship arrived in New York around the year 1700, and the young man quickly made an important place for himself in colonial society. He would have brought impressive letters of introduction and credit from Scotland. Shortly after his arrival in the colony he changed his name by adding the trailing 's', for reasons that have remained obscure to this day. This sort of thing was actually quite a common practice, befuddling researchers of every era. The father of the woman Robert was to marry in the New World spelled his family name variously as Nicholls, Nicoll and Nicholl.

In any case, Robert Watts had established himself well enough in the Province of New York by 1705 to be married to Mary Nicoll in December of that year, and marry well, he did. For Mary's mother Anna was born a Van Rensselaer, one of the most famous and powerful landowning families in North America. Mary's grandfather, Matthias Nicolls, had been part of the British expedition that had captured the colony from the Dutch and was the sixth Mayor of New York.

Her father, William, was a lawyer in the colony and Speaker of the Assembly for many years until 1718. William owned an estate of approximately 100 square miles in Islip on Long Island. William and Matthias may also have been related to Richard Nicholls, who became the first British Governor of the colony after he captured it from the Dutch in 1664.

The Van Rensselaers were, of course, of ancient Dutch origin. In the early 1600s, the colony had been *Nieuw* Amsterdam and was essentially owned by the Dutch West Indies Company, the VOC. The Company had granted a feudal title (patroonship) to the family, perhaps not surprising when one considers that Amsterdam pearl and diamond merchant Kiliaen Van Rensselaer was a founding Director of the VOC.

Their estate encompassed a stretch of land approaching *1,200* square miles, or roughly 740,000 acres, fronting on both sides of the Hudson River and surrounding Albany, New York. There seem to have been few, if any, negotiations with the previous owners of the land on the east side of the Hudson, but to the west, the Dutch for a time were valued allies of the Mohawk because they would supply weapons in exchange for furs, which aided the Iroquois in their wars with the French and the Hurons, and, after all, what's a few hundred thousand acres among friends?

The British captured the colony for the first time in 1665, but they left the great Dutch patroons with their rights to property and religion and they thus exerted enormous influence on regional affairs until long after the American Revolution. In the new United States of America, for instance, Anna's descendant Stephen Van Rensselaer became a member of the New York State Assembly in 1789 and Lieutenant Governor of the State in 1795. Fortune Magazine estimated him to have been the one of the ten richest Americans *of all time* in a 2007 article.

But, as if Robert's own credentials and his new connection by marriage to wealth and power were not enough, Mary Nicoll also happened to be granddaughter to Maria Van Cortlandt and, therefore, niece to another patroon, Stephanus Van Cortlandt. Stephanus had been granted a mere 86,000 acres on the Hudson below Albany and became the first native-born Mayor of New York City in 1677. His brother, Jacobus, also served two terms as Mayor during the early 1700s. Their mother was a Schuyler, another important family in the history of New York, whether it was Dutch colony, British province or American State.

It was to be expected, then, that ten years after Robert Watts' marriage, British colonial Governor Hunter proposed him to the board of the "Lords of Trade" of the City of New York in 1715. The Governor viewed him as, "a gentleman of sound sense, high respectability, large wealth and known affection to the Government." This traditional Watts family loyalty to the Crown was to survive dreadful trials in Jean Cruikshank's branch of the family, though not all of Robert Watts descendants remained loyal.

Robert's Dutch in-laws, on the other hand, were not so affectionate to the British, in spite of having retained such generous rights after British conquest. Van Rensselaers and Schuylers, not to mention Van Cortlandts, all figured prominently in the rebellion against the British Crown that became the American Revolution. Stephen Van Rensselaer was mentioned above. John Jay was Jacobus Van Cortlandt's grandson and he became the first Chief Justice of the United States of America. General Philip Schuyler was from Albany and became the initial commander of the American Congressional army forces that invaded Canada and captured Montreal in 1775. Schuyler was an inveterate foe of the Johnson family, which was also to be linked with the Watts by marriage a few years before the Revolution.

Those events lay far in the future, however, and 1715 was an auspicious year in Robert's personal life as well as his career, for the Watts' last child and only son and heir, John, was born on April 5th. Two of John's three older sisters appear to have returned, or been sent back to Scotland, and they died quite young, and unmarried. Father Robert may have gone back to visit Scotland in 1724, perhaps on the dismal mission to bury his eldest daughter in Edinburgh. According to one source, he had always intended to return to Scotland, but the death of his daughters there resulted in his remaining in America. The third daughter, Mary Watts, lived only to 23. She married but had just one son, who died in childhood.

John, born into wealth and priviledge, was also to become one of the most eminent lawyers in the province, and, like his father, rose very high in colonial society, until 1776. During the 1730s, as John grew up, the elite of New York society enjoyed a golden era, socializing and accumulating wealth. No war with France had threatened the expanding frontiers or threatened trade since 1713.

Men and women bearing other important names such as de Lancey, de Peyster, Alexander, Beekman as well as the oddly-named intellectual and outspoken physician, Cadwallader Colden, who was to publish a well-researched History of the Five Indian Nations – the first such book about the Iroquois — frequently partied at Robert Watts' home. Among this group of friends and visitors were several present and future Chief Justices and Governors of the Province.

But the curtain of history began to descend on this period during the early 1740s. First, the so-called War of Jenkins' Ear broke out in 1739 against Spain over slavery trade rights, after an English sea captain named Jenkins brandished his preserved ear in Parliament. His ear supposedly had been lopped off when a Spanish *garda-costa* vessel had stopped and boarded his ship on the Spanish Main. This had been a festering issue of international trade since the Treaty of Utrecht had granted Britain limited slave-trading access to the Spanish dominated Caribbean in 1713.

A severe winter in 1740 and '41 meant that the suffering of the poorer folk of the province reached unbearable levels, and suddenly New York society was terrified of a slave revolt. About one in five of the inhabitants of New York were black slaves in 1741, and after a number of suspicious fires occurred in the city, a suspected slave uprising was 'discovered' and brutally suppressed.

Robert Watts was foreman of the Grand Jury for the 1741 trial of suspected uprising conspirators. By the end of August 1741, thirteen slaves had been convicted and condemned. They were promptly and publicly burned at the stake *pour encourager les autres.* Seventeen more slaves and four white co-conspirators from the wrong side of the poverty line were hanged. Some modern historians tend to think that much of the case amounted to mere jumped-up hysteria, supporting the careerism of then-Governor Horsmanden. Contributing to the hysteria there had also been a recent slave uprising in South Carolina, and a previous revolt in New York in 1712. The mysterious fires ceased during the trials.

Generation Five

John Watts and Ann de Lancey

(1715-1789)

A year after the 1741 trials, Robert and Mary experienced a lovely contrast from the news of war abroad and grim doings at home. In July of 1742, their son, John, was now 27 and a rising star in the colony, and he married young Ann de Lancey, 19. No doubt John's father and mother were overjoyed, for not only was this a marriage into yet another pre-eminent New York family, but it brought new hope of continuing the Watts line, for by this time all of Robert's sisters had died.

"John Watts, from an oil painting in the family's possession"

"Ann de Lancey portrait courtesy of P.W. Watters through Ancestry.ca"

Ann was the third and youngest surviving daughter of Stephen (Étienne) de Lancey, a Huguenot immigrant from Caen, France. Stephen was the patriarch of the American de Lanceys, and had married Anne Van Cortland in 1700 in spite of arriving nearly penniless in the colony in 1686. He was a protestant French refugee, forced to flee after Louis XIV's revocation of the Edict of Nantes in 1685. At the time of Ann's marriage to Robert, Stephen was New York's Chief Justice. De Lancey had risen quickly to wealth and prominence and was an elected member of the New York Assembly for twenty-six years between 1702 and 1737. He donated the first town clock to New York City and, with business partner and later son-in-law John Watts, imported and presented the first fire engine to the city.

Stephen built a grand house on the corner of Pearl and Broad Streets in lower Manhattan in 1719, which has survived to become an enduring New York landmark called Fraunces' Tavern, in which many events of historical interest took place.[3]

"Fraunces' Tavern"

This de Lancey line can be traced directly back as far as one Guy deLancey, who was a *Viscompte* holding fiefdoms just south of the city of Laon, France, in 1432. Stephen's oldest son James, Ann de Lancey's brother, became a highly popular Lieutenant Governor of the province.

The war of Jenkins' Ear expanded into the War of the Austrian Succession, or King George's War, as it was known in the colonies. In 1744 Spain's ally France was inevitably but reluctantly entangled. Hostilities dragged on inconclusively until 1748. The Treaty of Aix-la-Chappelle was unpopular on all sides of the conflict, and on both sides of the Atlantic as well.

Many in the British colonies and in New France viewed it as merely an entr'acte to the inevitable final war with the French for possession of North America. The western penetration of an initial handful of British fur traders across the Appalachian Mountains into the Mississippi River watershed alarmed the French. The adventurous and doomed Sieur de la Salle had laid France's claim to the interior of North America some sixty years previously. They immediately began to construct a defensive chain of inland forts from Lake Erie to Louisiana.

The short-lived Treaty of Aix-la-Chappelle had also firmed up the beginnings of organized, disloyal sentiments towards the Crown in America, particularly in Boston. In an astonishing 1745 feat of arms, provincial troops and militia forces from Massachusetts, assisted by the Royal Navy, had captured the threatening French fortified harbour at Louisbourg on Cape Breton Island, Nova Scotia, (then, Ile Royale) after significant loss of life. But Britain had returned the enormous fortress to the French in the *status quo ante bellum* agreement of the 1748 treaty.

New Englanders felt abandoned and insulted, and sulked publicly that the Royal Navy had unfairly received the lion's share of the credit for the victory. The presence of the French naval base at Louisbourg continued to threaten their commerce and fisheries. That battle would have to be fought all over again, everyone knew.

The New York colony's support for King George's War against the French (aside from the Governor and a very few others, including outsider fur trader and Mohawk ally William Johnson, who had arrived from Ireland in 1737) had been feeble at best. The New Yorkers had become disenchanted with the war after terrible losses in the disastrous British attack on Spanish Cartagena in 1741, following which only 300 of 3,600 colonists had returned home, the rest dead from disease and starvation. The powerful Dutch fur trading families in Albany and their friends in the Assembly also much preferred to continue their lucrative trade with Montreal rather than go to war with New France.

Before the war had ended, John Watts purchased a farm of about 130 acres on Manhattan that extended from the East River across what is now Madison Square. It was bounded on the south by 21st Street and extended up what was then the Post Road to Boston. He named the farm Rose Hill, after the family's Scottish estate he had probably never seen, and he built a mansion there which had a "broad avenue lined with graceful elms" leading to it. The gateway was near the corner of 28th St. and Fourth Ave., and Bellevue Hospital is now on Rose Hill's original grounds.

He purchased this property from his brother-in-law, Provincial Chief Justice, James de Lancey. It was a portion of a farm originally owned by the Stuyvesant family. Like John's father's home, Rose Hill became a favourite summer gathering place and resort for the New York colonial aristocracy.

John's city house was near the waterfront, and became a well-known landmark. By then, John and Ann had a little boy, Robert, who was four, and two daughters; Ann, who was three and Susanna, who was an infant. Born in Rose Hill after 1747 were John (1749), Susanna (1751), Mary (nicknamed Polly) who was born in 1753, Stephen (born Christmas Eve, 1754) whose descendants include Jean Cruickshank and her children, Margaret (1755) and James (1756) who also died as a baby. The dynasty would assuredly continue, and now-grandfather Robert lived until 1750 to see at least some of his grandchildren begin their life journeys.

After the war, John's career and business continued to progress. The New-York Gazette records his election to the Provincial Assembly on November 13, 1752.

"Tuesday being the day appointed for the Election of a Representative to serve in the General Assembly, for the City and County of New York, in the room of Major Cornelius Vanhorne, deceased, John Watts, Esq. was unanimously chosen."

He is even mentioned in a local epic poem entitled, "On the DEATH of a late valorous and noble KNIGHT:" composed and published in 1752, on the news of the death of Royal Navy Admiral Warren in Ireland. The poem was an anonymous, lengthy, page three lament for the death of the Admiral, who had commanded the naval blockade and transported the Massachusetts troops to and from Louisbourg in 1745.

Admiral Warren had also married a de Lancey, and he was the uncle of William Johnson, whose star was beginning to rise rapidly. William Johnson and John Watts were to serve together on the Governor's Council for many years, and became very close.

" . . .
Him does each BRITON, in each clime, deplore;
But chief his widow's Wife, and INFANTS dear;
And thou, O YORK! His most distinguished Care,
With thy DE LANCEY'S, WATTS, thy Sons rever'd,
. . ."[4]   (caps from the original)

Extensive correspondence survives between John Watts and Johnson, until Johnson's death in 1774. In 1773, Watts' daughter, Polly (Mary), married Sir William's son, John.

"Polly Watts Johnson, Courtesy McCord Museum, Montreal, Canada"

John Watts' opinion was highly valued. He was one of six jurists selected by the province to defend its vaguely defined eastern boundaries against encroaching claims by neighbouring colonies of New Hampshire and Massachusetts. This was to be a highly contentious issue, particularly with respect to the New Hampshire "Grants" along the borderlands east of the Hudson River. A group of highly energetic and independent-minded folk led by one Ethan Allen and his clan continually stirred this pot.

Years later, during the American Revolution, the Allens threatened to go to war with both New York and New Hampshire individually and collectively, covertly negotiating with the British in Canada and flirting with proclaiming the neutrality of the Republic of Vermont!

They eventually founded the State of Vermont, which was carved mostly out of New Hampshire, perhaps attesting to the strength of New York's legal case, constructed in part by John Watts. Also in 1752, Watts helped fundraise and launched the Merchants' Exchange on Broad Street, the first trading exchange in the city's history. He was evidently a very public-spirited individual, for in 1753 he was one of twelve founding trustees of the New York Society Library. His name is on the charter granted to the Library by King George III in 1772.

In 1756 he was appointed to the Governor's (King's) Council at the behest of Governor Sir Charles Hardy and remained a member for twenty years, until it was dissolved at the outbreak of war with Britain. Also in 1756, a new war with France was declared, which would decide once and for all who would dominate North America. This followed 1754 wilderness skirmishes west of the Appalachians between the French and small British forces led by Major George Washington of the Virginia Provincial Regiment.

Ballooning into what Winston Churchill termed the real First World War, it brought tens of thousands of British troops through New York by the time Canada surrendered in 1760, and merchants there prospered, although the fur trade of the Albanians suffered. Anne's brother James de Lancey died suddenly that year. John Watts was summoned by a servant and found his brother-in-law dead in a chair. He later wrote, "had I not been appriz'd of it, I certainly should spoken [to him]."

But when the war ended, business in New York slumped, badly, and London at the same time began to try to recover some of the costs of the war from the colonies to reduce the enormous debt it had incurred. On the western side of the Atlantic this was, to say the least, unpopular. The cry of "No taxation without representation!" became a familiar refrain.

In 1762, during the early post-war period, John Watt continued his attachment to the Crown's interests, and became the personal attorney of Governor Monckton. His correspondence with the Governor during this period was considered to "present the best pictures of men and manners, politics and public feeling" prior to the American Revolution.[5]

Two years later, against colonial advice, including advice from John Watts, the British Parliament attempted to impose the revenue-raising Stamp Act. This led to outright rioting and mayhem right across the colonies in 1764-5. John Watts' friend Cadwallader Colden was acting Governor of the province at the time, after Monckton died in office. Colden was notoriously cantankerous on behalf of the Crown and in early 1765 rioters created an effigy of him, stole his elegant coach, smashed it and added them both to a great bonfire on Bowling Green.

John Watts was sincerely attached to the Crown, but his strong sense of natural justice had impelled him to defend the colonies when he thought that was the right thing to do. He joined New York's Committee of Correspondence, which was a hotbed of anti-Crown protests, and his "polished, witty and sarcastic" writing while a member of the Committee during this period was thought to have contributed significantly to the much-celebrated repeal of the Act in 1765 by Parliament.

This political stance by a member of the King's Council certainly did him no harm among New Yorkers, nor, it seems, with the Crown. According to one source, he "possessed a remarkably cheerful temper, which no disappointment could disturb, and a brain full of resources."[6] But gratitude and respect were all too short-lived.

John was elected Speaker of the Governor's Council, and he signed the address of the Council to Cadwallader Colden upon his re-appointment to Governor in 1769 – not London's most crowd-pleasing decision. And by now it was rapidly becoming less prestigious to be in the King's Party in New York or elsewhere in the colonies, other than in Nova Scotia and Quebec.

Also in 1769, the Watts celebrated the marriage of their second child, daughter Anne Watts (b. 1744) to Archibald Kennedy. Part of Anne's dowry is said to have been . . . Long Island! Kennedy was a widower, whose first wife had been a Schuyler, and had a significant pedigree of his own. He was a Captain in the Royal Navy, and was related to Scottish aristocracy, succeeding to the title of eleventh Earl of Cassilis (pronounced "Cassels") in 1792, shortly before he died. At that time Anne became the Countess of Casillis.

Kennedy had distinguished himself as a naval commander, having raised the siege of Lisbon in 1760, and the people of that city presented him with a handsomely engraved silver platter, which is still in the possession of the present Marquess of Ailsa. The earldom had originally been created in 1509 for the 3rd Lord Kennedy.

After he retired from the sea, Archibald lived in No. 1 Broadway, New York, but because of his refusal to take part in the Boston Tea Party, George Washington is supposed to have evicted him from his home and taken possession of it for himself. Archibald and Anne died in Scotland in 1794 and 1793, respectively. The ancient seats of the Earls of Cassilis included Culzean, Cullean, Cassilis and Newark Castles.[7][8]

"Ann Watts Kennedy, Countess of Cassilis, family portrait"

It is a very small world. Jean and her family have crossed paths more than once with Kennedy relatives quite unknowingly. As she recounted it,

"One [encounter was] early in the 20th century when Guy Johnson (brother of my grandmother, Sybil) stepped out the front door at Prince of Wales Terrace and bumped into his double. The two of them went inside to see if Guy's mother, Laight Johnson, could sort it out. The stranger was a Kennedy from Scotland, when he returned to Scotland he talked about his meeting. His mother confirmed the family connection and sent out the portrait of Anne Watts Kennedy, which we have in our living room. The second encounter was in the 1980's when a visiting head of school from Scotland, Norman Drummond, stayed with us in Lennoxville. We took him and his wife to our farm for a visit and when Elizabeth walked up our back staircase she was amazed to see a picture of Culzean Castle and the portrait of Anne Watts Kennedy. She asked what we were doing with those pictures. She pointed out the room she was born in and the fact that the woman is her ggggrandmother! So we are distantly related through her. Elizabeth's brother holds the title at the moment. Mother always said that the Kennedys needed the Watts money to refurbish Culzean!"

The Earl reportedly lost all of his American property, confiscated during the War of Independence. Likely, Archibald retained some other, more liquid assets, from his American real estate. When she died, Ann Watts Kennedy, Countess of Cassilis, was buried in the ruins of the royal Chapel of Holyrood, in Edinburgh, the customary residence of the Kings of Scotland before the Reformation. Several of those Kings are also interred there.

Public discourse continued to deteriorate in the British colonies in North America. In 1770, John Watts met with newly appointed Governor Dunmore during a meeting of his Council, held, perhaps significantly, in Manhattan's Fort George. At this meeting, the Governor ordered a specific, three-month term for follow-up to the awarding of land patents, to curb sharp practices and speculation in the province. The tone of this pronouncement from the Governor's Council meeting is choleric.

"It often happening after Grants of vacant lands . . . that the Petitioners delay . . . the Commencement of the Payment of Quit-Rents, whereby the Interest of the Crown is not only greatly prejudiced, but His Majesty's most gracious Intentions of promoting the Cultivation and Settlement of the Country obstructed . . ."

It was clear that ignorance of the law would not be accepted as an excuse.

" . . . that no person may pretend a Want of due Information in this Respect, the Clerk . . . is to cause a Copy of this Order to be constantly fixed up in the Secretary's Office and the same to be published, for six weeks consecutively, in one of the public News-Papers." [9]

That proclamation in its entirety was published on the front page of the paper. The time of trouble was coming, and discontent gathered strength in the colonies while polarization of feelings grew ever stronger.

As serious cracks began to appear in the social fabric, John's loyal adherence to the Crown became more noticeable. The New-York Gazette reported in March of that year that he had been present during the notoriously unpopular inquiries of the Governor and his Council into the activities of one Captain McDougall, who was imprisoned by the Crown for sedition after publishing an inflammatory paper called the Son of Liberty.

In the summer of 1770, John Watts' name appears again, this time on a published list of New York merchants opposed to non-importation boycotts of British goods to protest the Crown's imposition of duties. These names were to be remembered by patriots at some future day of reckoning.

Not all was totally grim, however. In October of 1770, one Peter Vianey advertised that he continued to be available to teach fencing and dancing (perhaps an odd-seeming combination, today) at Mrs. Hay's. The location was described as "opposite to the Hon. John Watts' house near the Exchange," another reference indicating the enduring familiarity of New Yorkers with his residence and person.

A month later, John Watts reached the pinnacle of his legal career and was confirmed as an attorney-at-law of the Supreme Court of New York. He continued to work for the betterment of his society. In 1771 he became President of the city's first hospital, which was granted a royal charter by George III in 1771. Although construction of the New York Hospital began in 1773, it was not completed and opened until long after the Revolutionary War was over. John Watts would never see it.

In 1773 he and Ann were able to enjoy the marriage of their twenty-year-old daughter Polly (Mary) to Sir John Johnson, soon-to-be heir to one of the largest estates in the province, that of John's old friend Sir William Johnson. Johnson had become a knighted war hero during the Seven Years' War and the Superintendent of Indian Affairs for the northern colonies. His estate was by that time vast, encompassing more than 250,000 acres in the Mohawk River Valley west of Albany.

King George himself had also made a baronet of his son, John. Sir William heartily approved of his son's marriage to Polly, as this link to a powerful New York family was far preferable to the disagreeable liaison Sir John had been conducting with an Albany Dutch farmer's daughter, Clarissa Putnam, by whom he had already fathered two children. Her life and descendants are beyond the scope of this book, but she did have a novel written about her!

Earlier, Sir John had described Polly as "an engaging lass, but at times her willfulness bedevils her beauty."[10] Perhaps that willfulness was her way of flirting, but it certainly remained a strong element of her personality for the rest of her life. A friend of Sir William described her as having, "Beauty, Good Sense, and a fine Personality,"[11] and another described her as, "a lady of great beauty, of the most amiable disposition, and composed of materials of the most soft and delicate kind."[12] That material was about to be severely tested.

The gathering political tsunami finally overwhelmed the colony. The Battle of Lexington on April 19, 1775 and the invasion of Canada later that year signaled the beginning of war. One by one, Loyalists on the lists of names being examined by Committees of Safety and Sons of Liberty found their number was up.

Generation Six

Stephen Watts and Sarah Nugent

(1754-1841)

Twenty-one-year-old Stephen was visiting his sister Polly at Johnson Hall when fighting broke out. This was the manor house in the Mohawk River Valley that her husband had inherited, the largest British house west of Albany. Sir William built it in 1763, when he was at the height of his fortune and power as Indian Superintendent for all the northern colonies.

"Photo of Johnson Hall"

While Stephen was there, Lieutenant-Colonel Allan Maclean was touring the region, disguised as a physician for safety reasons, since a British army officer could not risk travelling about the colony in uniform. He stayed at the Hall and recruited Stephen into his Loyalist Regiment, being formed largely from disbanded Scottish soldiers who had served in the Seven Years' War and who had settled in North America. Stephen became a Lieutenant in the First Battalion of the 84th Regiment of Foot, nicknamed the Royal Highland Emigrants.

This was the first American Loyalist regiment to be raised, and Stephen left Johnson Hall with Lt.-Col. Maclean in the spring of 1775, travelling west to Oswego on Lake Ontario, then down the St. Lawrence River to Montreal, eventually reaching Quebec City.

He was shortly to be followed by others fleeing the Mohawk Valley, among them Polly's cousin by marriage Guy Johnson, who had become Superintendent of Indian Affairs upon the death of her father-in-law. Guy Johnson and 200 others, including Mohawk War Chief Joseph Brant, British Indian Department employees, his own wife, and other friends and family of the Johnsons arrived at Oswego in June, and travelled downriver to Montreal. Guy's wife, Mary, died in childbirth at Oswego during that journey.

Guy and Joseph Brant disagreed with the actions of Sir Guy Carleton, Military Governor of Canada, in the early stages of the war. Still hoping for reconciliation with the rebels, Carleton had prohibited Indian warfare, and so Johnson and Brant travelled to London to lobby for their position. Carleton was already no particular fan of the Johnson clan, disliking merchants as a class in general, and this action, in direct defiance of his order for them to proceed to Fort Niagara, did nothing to improve their reputation in his mind.

As war intensified and expanded, Polly and Sir John Johnson clung to each other and to their home in Johnson Hall through a very trying winter, also hoping against hope for reconciliation between the colonists and Britain. But the spring of 1776 would bring an end to their time together in the Mohawk Valley.

The Americans attacked and captured Montreal in the summer of '75 and then proceeded down the St. Lawrence River in an attempt to complete the annexation and 'liberation' of Canada by capturing Quebec City. Lt. Stephen Watts served with small elements of the 84th during Carleton's successful defense of Quebec City against American attack and siege in the winter of 1775/6 – the first defeat suffered by Congressional forces. He likely served under Captain John Nairne and during the American attack on Quebec City New Year's Eve, 1775, a counter attack by Captain Nairne's company, including a bayonet charge, entrapped the Americans killing some 50 with over 400 surrendering. General Benedict Arnold was wounded in the leg, but escaped. Stephen then participated in chasing the American army out of Canada, after General Burgoyne arrived with reinforcements, and in the late spring of 1776, he was encamped with the 84th in the vicinity of Montreal.

By then his father, John, had been forced to flee for his life from New York. On the night of April 5, 1775, apparently after some of John's letters to London (no doubt as acerbic as usual but in this instance critical of the rebels) were intercepted and read aloud before an excitable mob in one of the New York coffee houses. The rioters then attacked the Watts' well known downtown home, emboldened by the arrival of Continental troops under General Putnam in the city a few days earlier.

According to a story in the Livingston family archives, included in Welles' history of the Watts family, John's friend Robert R. Livingston, a fellow judge with strongly republican views, had been able to distract the mob by his eloquence until John and Ann could escape into hiding. John left her behind in New York a month later, went into exile, and never saw her again.

"I embarked in the Charlotte packet 4th May, and left the lighthouse at seven in the morning following, with a heavy heart, foreseeing the distresses that were hanging over us."[13]

Whether that tale of gallant rescue by Livingston is true or not, John and Ann, and some of their offspring, but not all, experienced a nightmarish and heartbreaking fall from grace that appears to have killed Ann, for she survived his departure to exile only two months, dying in New York on July 3, 1775.

The Watts family, like many others, was ripped apart. Leading up to the war, one can only imagine what family gatherings were like. Perhaps the rule of no politics and no religion during dinner prevailed. Perhaps they made a pact, as others certainly did, that no matter who won the struggle, someone in the family would be on the winning side.

Certainly, sons Robert and John remained in New York and prospered after their parents fled, as did daughters Anne and Susanna. John, in particular, rose to prominence as Speaker of the New York State Assembly in 1791, and was later elected to Congress. Robert had been a founder of the New York Chamber of Commerce in 1768.

John lived on in exile in Britain until 1789, but there is no evidence he returned to Edinburgh and he seems to have become resigned to his fate. A white marble monument was erected to his memory in the Nave south wall of medieval St. Olave's Church on Hart Street in London, at the corner of Seething Lane – making it a reasonable assumption that he is buried there, as one reliable source indicates, although other sources have him buried in various other places, including Wales. There had originally been a Watts coat of arms on the monument, but that disappeared in 2007.[14] [15] [16]

"Monument to John Watts in St. Olave's Church, London, Nave South Wall. Courtesy of Monumental Inscriptions and Heraldry in St Olave's, Hart Street, London, with annotations from wills, etc. *transcribed and annotated by Arthur J. Jewers, and edited and indexed by A. W. Hughes Clarke, 1929; originally published in* Miscellanea Genealogica et Heraldica.*"*

His son, Stephen, was later to follow him to be interred there. It is unclear why St. Olave's, an ancient London church dedicated to the patron saint of Norway, might have become their church. Perhaps it was the church of exiles. Famed Diarist and Secretary of the Royal Navy Board in the 1600s Samuel Pepys is also buried there. Elizabeth I gave thanks there upon her release from the Tower.

The de Lancey family was similarly affected. Most of the family remained loyal, but some did not. Oliver Warren de Lancey at the age of 15 was part of the British Army assault on Chatterton Hill during the Battle of White Plains in 1776. Stephen Ross Watts later related, "While the British were advancing up the hill a shot struck one of the standard bearers dead. Warren instantly seized the colours – rushing forward was one of the first to gain the summit, where he planted them in the ground. For this act of bravery he received a coronet's commission from Sir William Howe."

A grandson of Oliver's, Sir Wm. Delancey, fought as Quarter Master General with Wellngton at the Battle of Waterloo and was killed there, his loss lamented by the Duke in his official report which states, " . . . I had every reason to be satisfied with the conduct of . . . Col. Delancey, who was killed by a cannon shot in the middle of the action. This officer is a serious loss to his majesty's service, and to me at this moment."

As the revolution ground on, New York State confiscated the estates of John Watts without compensation, as revolutionaries are fond of doing in any era and place, whether in the United States of America or Cuba. This Act of Attainder of October 22, 1779, also banished John Watts (and a list of others, including Sir John Johnson, Royal Governors and several other Supreme Court Justices) on pain of death.

The city house on Pearl Street burned in 1776, lost in the great fire that destroyed much of New York City following the defeat and withdrawal of the American army from the city that year. Patriot sons John and Robert were able to repurchase the properties from the State, and John's father's will eventually also left them to Robert, the eldest son.

Eldest son Robert's first surviving daughter was born at Rose Hill in the 1770s and at least two other daughters were born there as well. By 1881 what remained of the estate had descended to Union Army officer John Watts de Peyster, grandson of John Jr.'s daughter Mary Justina Watts, who had married Frederick de Peyster. Frederick would be a participant in events that further sundered the family.

But Polly had married Sir John Johnson, and her younger brother, Stephen, was now a British soldier. They, and the rest of the colonial Loyalists were now in a very personal fight to the death with enemies of the crown. In late spring of 1776, Sir John was forced to set out on foot with 170 other Loyalists through the trackless Adirondack Mountains a few hours ahead of an arrest order. His companions are often dismissed as 'retainers' or 'tenants', but many of these men were Catholic Scottish Highlanders, veterans of the Scottish wars, whom Sir John's father had brought over and settled around Johnstown, Their new Lairds had won their respect, and the patriots had not. In fact, the patriots hated and feared the warlike potential of Johnson's Catholic "tenants" to the extent that by this time several of the their chieftains had been taken hostage and jailed in Albany as sureties for the rest of their clan's behavior.

The arresting force of 300 blue-coated Continental soldiers of the 3rd New Jersey Regiment arrived at Johnson Hall a few short hours after Polly's husband had left. A friend had tipped him off that the army was on the march for Johnson Hall. Polly stoutly and effectively misled the soldiers as to her husband's intentions, and was immediately arrested and taken under guard to Albany. There, she and her two children were held hostage for her husband's behavior on pain of death, and in Albany she gave birth to a son, their third child, while their estate was being looted. This son was always sickly, and died young. Sir John always blamed his ill health on the treatment of his wife during this time.

Johnson and his starving band emerged from the forests southwest of Montreal after a dreadful three-week hike across the mountains in late spring. His Indian guides got lost, and the group subsisted on bark and sprouting beech leaves for the final ten days. Four days after they arrived, British Military Governor Sir Guy Carleton, authorized Sir John to take the rank of Lieutenant-Colonel and form the King's Royal Regiment of New York, on June 19, 1776, but left it to his subordinate John Burgoyne to communicate that Sir John's regiment would have to be raised, equipped and paid out of Sir John's own pocket, and was considered a Fencible regiment, a step below the American Provincial regiments of the regular army, such as Allan MacLean was forming.

This was not uncommon, but Burgoyne's was the first in a long series of apparent slights and snubs that Sir John was to endure until the end of his life at the hands of British authorities. Similar treatment had factored strongly in George Washington's decision to take up the rebel cause.

Stephen was in the area with the 84th, heard that his brother-in-law had arrived, and transferred to Sir John's regiment. He is recorded as joining the regiment on the first day of its existence, although he was apparently still officially on the payroll of the 84th some time later.[17]

Sir John promoted him to Captain, and gave him command of the Light Infantry Company of the First Battalion, KRRNY. The "Light Bobs" as they were known, were the mobile scouts and skirmishers of the army, deployed in advance of the line infantry companies of the regiment in order to detect, harass, disorganize and slow down the enemy. After a year of organization and training, a chance to hit back at the rebels came their way.

General John (Gentleman Johnnie) Burgoyne had lobbied successfully over the winter in London to be given overall command of forces that he believed would swiftly end the war. London promoted him over the head of his senior officer, General Carleton, provoking Carleton's request to resign. Burgoyne's plan was to march south from Montreal and capture Albany. General, Lord Howe, was to march his army north from New York to meet him, and a third force under Brigadier Barry St. Leger was to attack from the west towards Albany as well, down the Mohawk River Valley. Success in this campaign would split the northern from the southern colonies and end the war.

Sir John Johnson's Yorkers formed part of the latter force, and in early August, St. Leger began a siege of the American garrison at Fort Stanwix, at the height of land near the headwaters of the Mohawk River, about halfway to Albany from Lake Ontario.

On August 6, 1777, mixed forces under Sir John Johnson's command successfully ambushed a relief column of Tryon County militia roughly twice their size, at a crossing of Oriskany Creek. This was the bloodiest battle of the Revolutionary War. During six hours of vicious hand-to-hand fighting between former Mohawk Valley neighbours, Stephen led a bayonet charge of the Light Infantry in an attempt to break into the American defensive position, and later participated in a second assault on the surrounded American militia. A musket ball shattered one leg, he was bayoneted through the windpipe, and was reported to have had a third wound as well.

Stephen was left for dead when the Loyalist forces withdrew to the fort, having killed or wounded about 500 of the Americans — more than half the column. British losses were significantly smaller, at about 160 killed and wounded. After the battle, an American soldier, Private Henry Failing, carried the terribly wounded Captain Watts down to the bank of Oriskany creek where he was able to drink, and Stephen gave the soldier his bull's-eye pocket watch in gratitude. Apparently Failing later sold the watch for $300.00. Two days later, Stephen was discovered still alive by two British-allied Indian scouts, who brought him back to the camp, where his lower leg was amputated successfully.

The Loyalists had won a clear tactical victory at Oriskany by slaughtering and turning back the relief column, but St. Leger failed to capture Fort Stanwix, anyway, mostly due to not bringing siege artillery from Montreal. He had ignored colonial scouts' reports and advice about recent strengthening of the fort.

Weeks later, Burgoyne's army was surrounded and forced to surrender at Saratoga, after General Howe decided he would take his large army off to attack Philadelphia instead of participating in Burgoyne's New York campaign.

Saratoga was the turning point of the war, and France recognized the United States upon hearing of the victory. Burgoyne was never given another significant command, although historians now tend to hang responsibility for this defeat higher up, on the shoulders of Lord George Germain, Minister for the Colonies, who seems to have forgotten to give any direction to Lord Howe regarding supporting Burgoyne during the Campaign of 1777.

Having failed in the north, British strategy was to shift offensive operations to the south, and for the next year or two, Loyalists were used mostly in labour battalions, chopping firewood and reinforcing fortifications. Stephen returned to Montreal, and in January of 1778 he is listed as "sick" on the roll of the KRRNY. In March of that year, he purchased a commission as Captain in the regular army 8th Regiment of Foot and was put in command of a hospital in Montreal.

In September, the army recommended he be sent to England for hot baths, to recover the flexibility of the knee on his injured leg so that he could make use of an artificial leg. In 1780 Parliament voted him 100 pounds for the cure of his wound and by December of 1781 he had taken up command of an invalid Company of the Veterans' Regiment on the Isle of Jersey in the English Channel. I

"Major Stephen Watts, 3rd Battalion, Royal Veterans Regiment. Image courtesy of Janeen Soderling, New Zealand."

EXTRACT: GENERAL FREDERICK HALDIMAND TO LORD BARRINGTON

Sorel 1 October 1778
The bearer, Captain Watts of the 8th Regiment, returns to England for the benefit of the hot baths to recover the flexibility of the joint of his knee to enable him to use an artificial leg. The Regiment being to send home an officer for their additional company in the room of those who came to Canada last year, I have proposed to Your Lordship in my public dispatch of the 27th Ultimo that he should serve in that company for the Captain, which will prevent the Regiment from being obliged to send another also. Captain Watts served in Sir John Johnson's Corps at the action last summer on the Mohawk River where the rebels were defeated with so great a slaughter by the Five Nations and a part of that Corps commanded by Sir John Johnson in person. Captain Watts received three dangerous wounds and lay some days in the woods without assistance, was discovered only by accident, and has recovered after a tedious and painful confinement with the loss of a leg cut off below the knee, which he is not yet able to support himself upon. Sir Guy Carleton, in consideration of Captain Watts being of a family in New York which has suffered much in these troubles, and brother-in-law of Sir John Johnson whose merits must be known to Your Lordship, but principally on account of his gallantry at the action above mentioned, and his fortitude in the suffering he underwent, allowed him at his earnest instance to purchase a company which was to be sold in the 8th Regiment, which circumstances I thought merited to be made known to Your Lordship.[18]

On Jersey, he met Sarah Nugent, and they were married at St. Helier in 1788, when she was 17. During their life together, they had fourteen children, and Jean Cruickshank and her children are descended from one of them, Robert Nugent Watts. Robert's sister, Anne, was born in 1804, and married a Charles J. de Belin, whose direct descendant, Les de Belin, lives in 2014 in Australia and contributed significantly to the story of Stephen in these pages.

"Sarah Nugent"

Sarah Nugent was from a family that had immigrated to Jersey from Clonlost, Westmeath, Ireland. There, the Nugents were important people – the name is attached to aristocrats and landowners descended from knights that arrived with William the Conqueror, and there were various clans of them, some dedicated to freeing Ireland from the yoke of England and others taking the part of the British. Unfortunately, the exact connection between Sarah and the Westmeath Nugents is not yet clear.

According to handwritten family lore, Sarah's grandfather was named Packenham Nugent, was born about 1695, and was grand-uncle, perhaps by marriage, to one Lord Longford, who was the Captain of a Royal Navy warship. Nugent married a woman named Anne Smith of Kiltomb, who was the widow of a prominent person named Packenham, also from Westmeath. I have been unable to track down any other record of a Packenham Nugent, although Packenham is certainly an illustrious name in Royal Navy history, and the Longford estate is located right in Westmeath.

In any case, the pair ended up in Jersey and had a number of children, including Sarah's father, Walter Nugent (b. 1730 in Jersey), who became a Fort Major and Adjutant in the 75th Regiment of the British Army. Walter Nugent married Esther Bandinel in 1761. Esther was the daughter of Philip Bandinel the Seigneur de Meleshes, another ancient and pedigreed family, so the Nugent connection likely was an important one, for families concerned with bloodlines. Sarah was born ten years later.

Sarah had three sisters and a younger brother, Walter, who was killed in action with the British Army in India. In 1783 one sister, Ann Susanne, married Dr. Roger Heriot of Ladykirk, Scotland, which is east of Edinburgh. Heriot had been transferred to Jersey in February of 1783 as Surgeon to the Forces. That turned out to be a fortunate connection for Stephen, for despite the undoubted happiness ensuing from his wedding and his growing and evidently loving family, he had a quotient of suffering yet to endure.

He was appointed Barrack Master in Jersey eight years later, but in November of 1796 dueled with the Paymaster of the Regiment over lodging money allowed to officers. Stephen fired first, grazing his opponent's neck, but his opponent then shot away Stephen's right thumb, the ball then entering his nose, to lodge, inoperably, in his cheekbone. Stephen was expected to die, but eventually survived thanks to the attentions of brother-in-law Roger Heriot. Roger and Anne's son Frederick George Heriot would later move to Canada, followed by Robert Nugent Watts and his brother Gordon.

It is curious that the Watts and Heriot families were joined here in Jersey, and again in Canada, and it hints once more that they may well have known each other in Edinburgh two hundred years before. The Edinburgh Heriots are famous — George Heriot was goldsmith to James VI, to whom John Watt was also well known, and endowed a famous hospital in the city.[19] The Heriot-Watt University founded there in 1821 offers more intriguing evidence of close family ties, although in this case it appears to be just coincidence, for James Watt, the great inventor that the University name commemorates seems not directly related to the Watt family of Edinburgh that emigrated to America.

There seems not to be much in the way of actual documentary evidence related to which branch of the Heriots moved to Jersey. Sources suggest that Frederick George Heriot's antecedents were of the Ladykirk, Shiels and Berwickshire branches of the Heriots, but available records are inconclusive. One source indicates that the Jersey Heriots were a "cadet branch" of the Heriots of Trabroun, who go back to 1423 in that place, the land being granted to John Heriot for military service by Archibald, Earl of Douglas. [20] [21]

Duels in the British Army were illegal, but Stephen appears not to have been charged, and he continued in his army career even though his second fled the country. In 1799, when his son Stephen Ross was born, he held the rank of Major while in the Island service, and the position of Assistant Barrack-Master-General. But ten years later, in December 1809, a newspaper article reported "Captain Stephen Watts on the retired list, and late of the 3rd Royal Veteran Battalion is dismissed from his Majesty's Service."

This may have led to his suicide, although there is no apparent reason given for the dismissal. Perhaps it was belated punishment for participating in the duel. Shortly after the announcement, on January 20, 1810, he shot himself in the head in London, and died. A Colonel Frank suggested at the inquest into the death that Major Watts was liable to occasional fits of insanity.[22] One might well imagine he could be, with a lead ball embedded in his cheekbone for more than a decade!

Stephen was buried in the crypt of St. Olave's Church, London, near his father John, on January 24, 1810. The crypt was filled in by rubble after 1850, when such burials were outlawed, and the church survived firebombing in 1941 during the German air attacks on London. Sarah survived him for many years, and there is a memorial plaque to them at Ripple Church, Deal, Kent. Sarah was originally buried in St. Leonard's, but reburied in Ripple Church, where their surviving children placed the plaque. Stephen's daughter in-law Mary Anne (married to Stephen Ross Watts, who recorded a great deal of the Watts family line) was the youngest daughter of the Rector of Ripple Church, Charles Philpot.[23]

Generation Seven

Robert Nugent Watts and Charlotte Sheppard

(1806-1882)

Robert Nugent Watts was one of the children who placed the plaque. He was born on Jersey in 1806, but according to one family letter, he and brother Charles were living in Bath in the early 1820s and were sent off to Sproston's School in 1823. Four years later he immigrated to Lower Canada, settling in Quebec City and the town of Drummondville in the region known as the Eastern Townships, southeast of Montreal. The Townships were at the time being settled mostly by English-speaking immigrants from Britain, but since have gradually become largely French in character. This began a long and deep connection to Canada for Jean Cruickshank's family.

Robert was already well connected from Jersey when he arrived, for in 1802 his distinguished cousin, bachelor Frederick George Heriot, had preceded him. This may have been a motivating factor for Robert's emigration. Frederick had arrived in Canada as a 16-year-old Ensign in the 49th Regiment of Foot under the command of General Sir Isaac Brock.

Heriot had an illustrious career with the army in Canada during the War of 1812, following which he accepted a 600-acre land grant and retired to found the town of Drummondville in 1815 instead of being redeployed with the Army. Heriot had served under Lt. Col. de Salaberry as a Major in the famous *Régiment des Voltigeurs Canadiens*, and led four companies of the Voltigeurs from Montreal to defend Kingston in 1813. Navy Commodore Yeo mentioned him in dispatches for the role he played in the amphibious raid on the headquarters of the American Lake Ontario fleet at Sackett's Harbour, and Adjutant-General Byrnes stated in his report that

" . . . two companies of Canadian Voltigeurs commanded by Major Heriot . . . evinced the most striking proofs of their loyalty, steadiness and courage." [24]

Heriot also won high praise at the brilliant Canadian victories at the Battle of Chateauguay and Crysler's Farm later that year.

Frederick ended his military career as a Major-General, having purchased command of the Voltigeurs from de Salaberry. He was appointed a Companion of the Bath in 1822 and served as aide-de-camp to the Governor of Quebec. By 1838 he had accumulated about 12,000 acres around Drummondville.[25]

When Robert Nugent Watts arrived in Quebec he found a position in the colony as an assistant in the office of the Civil Secretary for Lower Canada, doubtless with Frederick's influence and assistance, which may well have also extended to Robert's older brother Gordon who ended up as a clerk in the Military Secretary's office in Quebec City. At some point Robert purchased some land, doubtless from his cousin, and he settled near Heriot in Drummondville and took up farming, including horse breeding.

Robert met and married Charlotte Sheppard in Quebec City in 1839, when Charlotte was 23. Robert and Charlotte had six children in Drummondville and Jean is a descendant of their daughter Laight Elizabeth Sarah Watts, who was born on October 8, 1840.

Charlotte's father, William Sheppard, was a timber merchant and ship owner who also had connections to both Drummondville and the Government in Quebec City. He was born in Edinburgh in 1784, and had arrived in Canada with his father at the age of twelve. In England, the Sheppard line is traceable back into Yorkshire history quite far; in one account there are deeds as far back as 1529.

By 1809 William had become a successful businessman and that year he married Henrietta Harriet Campbell, daughter of the King's Notary, Archibald Campbell, in Quebec City. Campbell was a Loyalist who had come to Canada following the American Revolution. The Campbells similarly have a long, traceable lineage, which is not within the scope of this book to follow up. A niece of Harriet's, Margery Durham Campbell, related that,

"We loved Uncle Sheppard, but were rather in awe of our aunt, who was very clever, quick to see faults, gay and kind-hearted; a botanist and a naturalist. She wrote a little article on the Birds of Canada in the Transactions of the 'Literary and Historical Society of Quebec.' She tried to make out that there were beautiful song birds in Canada. I fear that she had not a good case."

William established the village of Sheppardville, which became Bergerville and is now Sillery, just west of Quebec City, after buying a large old French estate there, which he greatly expanded and named Woodfield. The original building us described by niece Margery as,

" . . . a fine old French building, with a round staircase, and a gallery at the top leading to the bedrooms; a room downstairs called the saloon, next to a large drawing room; dining room, library and an aviary full of lively well-cared-for birds. On the other side of the saloon was a charming little breakfast room; the back of the house looked over the river. It was a paradise for us children." [26]

That building burned one Christmas, and William and Charlotte built a second one on the site. Sheppard laid out the town of Sheppardville, and named a number of streets in it after family members (not excluding himself)! Granddaughter Laight has an avenue named for her that exists to this day about a half mile west of the Yacht Club de Québec.

"The Honorable William Shepherd"

Sheppard had partnered with brother-in-law John Saxton Campbell in the timber business, and was said to have been involved in the construction of the side-wheel steamship *Royal William* in Quebec, which, in 1833, became the first vessel to travel across the Atlantic entirely under steam power (except for when she stopped to clean her boilers.) It appears that they had to burn the ship's rails and furniture to keep steam up. *Royal William* was constructed for the Quebec and Halifax Steam Navigation Company, whose shareholders included Black, Samuel Cunard, and other prominent Lower Canadians.[27] [28] [29] Unfortunately, she turned out to be a losing investment, after she was quarantined during a cholera epidemic.

"Old Woodfield. Sarah Watts is the largest child."

In the turbulent year of 1837 armed revolt broke out in both Upper and Lower Canada. That year Sheppard was appointed to the Executive Council of Lower Canada, and served there until Upper and Lower Canada were united as Canada East and Canada West in 1841, although he appears to have been a reluctant politician.

He and Charlotte's mother were very well known and active in Quebec society, and both of them were naturalists who presented papers to the Literary and Historical Society of Quebec. Sheppard, his father-in-law Archibald Campbell, and Governor-General Lord Dalhousie, had helped organize the Society and Sheppard was its president for many years between 1831 and 1847.

In 1847 disaster overtook the Canadian lumber trade due to a reduction in British preferential tariffs. A financial panic was followed by a worldwide depression. William Sheppard suffered very serious financial losses, and was forced to sell Woodfield and retire to his estate at Drummondville, which was known as Fairymeade.

"Fairymeade"

Nearly a century later, Woodfield had become the cemetery for St. Patrick's Church, perhaps a fitting fate for it, since the cargo holds of Canadian lumber ships were used to bring nearly 100,000 starving Irish back to Canada after the terrible potato famine of 1846. Tens of thousands died of typhus and other diseases during and after the ocean passages.

A sympathetic administration appointed William to the position of Major in the Drummondville Militia Regiment in 1847, and he eventually became a Lt-Col. In 1859, he submitted recommendations regarding the militia to the Governor General. William Shepherd died suddenly in 1867. Two days before his death, he wrote an affectionate letter to his granddaughter Charlotte, nicknamed Chatty, which has survived.

Robert Nugent Watts, on the other hand, was considerably more interested in politics than his father-in-law, and with the support of his cousin Heriot he was duly elected to the first Legislative Assembly for the United Province of Canada (capital, Kingston) on March 15, 1841, as the Conservative member for the riding of Drummond, Canada East.

The first three sessions of the First Parliament of Canada were held in newly built Kingston General Hospital. The present magnificent Kingston City Hall was constructed to serve as the capital of Canada, although by the time it was finished the Government had moved the seat of Parliament and it would never actually meet in the new building.

Great things were afoot and a letter from Robert to Frederick, who acted as his returning officer, provides an interesting glimpse into the first Parliament of Canada on July 24, 1841.

"We had a sharp debate last night in the House on the propriety of paying the Members. I was called to order for calling them pillagers of their constituents' money and told them so many unpleasant truths they would not let me finish but coughed me down. These resolutions were carried and referred to a committee. I called for a division and stood up alone protesting against the measure."

Robert was re-elected when the capital was moved to Montreal for the 2nd Parliament in 1844 and re-elected a third and final time to the 3rd Parliament in 1848 – 1851, during which period the capital moved again, to Toronto (after the Montreal House was burned to the ground by disgruntled Montreal Tory merchants).

Of course, in those days before the secret ballot, winning often depended more on how much whisky you provided the boys than what your platform was. Family anecdotes provide other insights into political tactics of the day,

"All the ex-soldiers backed [Robert] and didn't leave anything to chance. One time, voters had to go by train to cast their ballots. The engineer was Conservative, so according to plan they stopped the train a mile or two before the station, picked up the conservative voters and rushed by the station without stopping. Another time the liberals commandeered the polling station, which was in a hardware store . . . . the conservatives arrived, grabbed axe handles and evicted the liberals. R.N. Watts won again."

Robert was a colleague of Sir John A. Macdonald's during the second and third parliaments, although party discipline was nothing like it is today, and he probably was one of the Conservative members that Macdonald wryly referred to as "loose fish." He seems, in fact, to have become friends with a Reform Party MPP from Canada West, Malcolm Cameron, and there are two letters to him from Cameron that have survived.

Robert also became a Lt.-Colonel in the Canadian militia. His cousin Frederick invited the couple to live in his home in Drummondville for several years, and they eventually inherited the entire estate that cousin Frederick called Comfort Cottage, when cousin Frederick was carried off by typhus in 1843. Robert by then was quite well-to-do from his farming — one had to own property in those days even to vote, much less become a Member of Parliament, and bachelor Frederick had no children.

Daughter Laight Elizabeth was born there on October 8, 1840. Shortly after Frederick's death, Robert replaced Comfort Hall with a lovely limestone manor house they named Grantham Hall, where he and Charlotte brought up their family.

"Comfort Cottage"

In a letter to her mother from there in June of 1844, Charlotte tartly expresses a bit of wifely disapproval of her husband's busyness, suggesting Harriet come to Drummondville from Woodfield to relieve her rheumatism because,

"Nugent is too busy looking after his farm and road to leave D'ville even for a week and retain the character of minding his business so you are not to expect him this summer –see how he has crushed our bright plans by a few strokes of his [pen] . . ."

"Watercolour of Grantham Hall"

During this period, according to preserved family letters and documents from the late 1830s and '40s, the death of John Watts (Jr.), the uncle of Robert Nugent Watts and Charles Watts, in September, 1836, led to family disputes, fraud and tragedy involving his New York estate, which included the property purchased following confiscation by the State from his father, John (Sr.) during the Revolution, and then subsequently inherited when John (Sr.) died in Britain.

John (Jr.) was the last Recorder of New York City under the Crown. Unlike Stephen, he and brother Robert joined the patriots. They did not follow their father into exile, or younger brother Stephen into war against the rebels, but remained in New York during the Revolution, there to prosper. John became the Speaker of the New York State Assembly from 1791-93, then was elected to Congress for a term, and was appointed the first judge of Westchester County. His son, Robert, inherited a large estate from an uncle by marriage, but predeceased his father. John then endowed an orphanage with that money, for which act a statue to him was erected on the grounds of Trinity Church. He married his cousin, Jane de Lancey, in 1774.

The executors of John Watts's estate were two sons-in-law. Frederick de Peyster and Philip Kearny, Sr. De Peyster had married John's daughter Mary Justina Watts in 1820. Kearny, a prominent and wealthy New York financier, had married Susan Watts, who died young in 1822.

The collection of family letters related to this event spans nearly ten years from 1837 to 1846 and involves Robert Nugent Watts, his brothers Gordon and Charles, cousins P.J. Kearny and Frederick de Peyster, Gordon's friend, S. Macaulay, and a business partner named Bell.

The Kearnys were a large clan, and some of the Kearnys alive during this period went on to become celebrated American military heroes — Major-General Phil Kearny, Philip Sr.'s son, was killed during the retreat following the second Union defeat at Bull Run in 1862 and another Major Kearny was killed at Gettysburg the year following. A third soldier, Major-General Stephen Watts Kearny became Military Governor of California in 1846 following a successful campaign against Spain in Mexico. But Financier Philip Sr. also had one less-than-successful nephew, Philip John Kearny, who will be referred to hereafter as P.J. Kearny.

Gordon Watts had settled in Quebec City, where he had met and married a young Englishwoman, Mary Sponge from Sandgate, Kent, in 1833. Upon notification of Uncle John's death, he, along with brother Charles back in Jersey, accepted the apparently kind offer of New York cousin P.J. Kearny to be their local financial agent. Young P.J. reinvested Gordon's entire $11,000 inheritance from Uncle John Watts and the interest accruing on Charles' inheritance in the New York stock market, just weeks before it collapsed in 1837 from a decade of wild speculation in western land purchases and railways.

It's not clear how P.J. Kearny came to be recommended to Gordon and Charles Watts as a reliable financial agent, but P.J. himself asserted his investments were all made with the approval of his wealthy Uncle Phil. Later, Frederick de Peyster was to write that it was a pity no one had acquainted Gordon with the actual nature of P.J.'s investments. Indeed it was. Perhaps uncle Philip Kearny Sr. wanted his nephew to learn the ropes. John Watts' overall estate was worth millions of 1836 dollars, so encouraging P.J. to dabble in the overheated market with a few thousand of someone else's money may have seemed like a good idea at the time.

Sadly, beginning their ill-fortune, in June of 1837, Gordon and Mary lost the third of their three children to that time, four-year-old son, John Stephen. Mary was then already pregnant with their fourth child. It appears that she and Gordon travelled to England that summer, perhaps to visit family. One can well imagine that after losing three children in four years, they might have decided that a vacation was in order, possibly also financed by the exhilarating prospect of inheriting a small fortune.

Mary did not return to Canada with her husband, and their daughter, Sarah, was born in Brussels, in August. Perhaps she stayed overseas for a time against Gordon's wishes, for a curious reference to her appears in a letter to Gordon from brother Charles the following summer, " . . . I hope Mary has behaved better of late." Possibly Gordon heard about the collapse of the New York financial system while he was in Britain, or he may have been summoned home because of the looming political crises in Upper and Lower Canada.

At any rate, from the correspondence it appears that, as P.J.'s investments burned, he decided the only way to restore his situation was to throw more money into the volcano. He asked Gordon for a loan and Gordon foolishly then tossed good money after bad, loaning P.J. an additional $6000, (not to mention a couple of $100 gifts to P.J.'s children) in the summer of 1837. This particular investment was supposedly secured by a mortgage on P.J.'s part-ownership in some rental property in New York, and all this apparently also had the blessing of Uncle Phil.

Since Gordon was just a clerk at the time, probably paid only the equivalent of a few hundred

about the additional loan, de Peyster wrote to Gordon, P.J.'s uncle Phil had guaranteed that sum on behalf of his nephew.

By December of 1839 it had become all too clear; the inheritance and Gordon's loan were gone for good. One letter indicated P.J. Kearny had formed the intention to relocate to a farm in Wisconsin, on the far northwestern frontier.

It all proved too much to bear. Just over a month later, on February 4, 1840, Stephen committed suicide in his residence in the old town of Quebec City. To the additional horror of his friends and family his death was followed the next day by that of his distraught wife, Mary. Their last surviving child, three-year-old daughter Sarah, was left penniless and orphaned. No account indicates where she was when her mother and father killed themselves. Robert and Charlotte took the little girl in, of course, and raised her in what seems to have been a very loving environment. Two silver christening cups bearing the names of the daughters of Gordon and Mary Watts are mute testimony to those tragic days.

But even then, the terrible story was not over. An unpleasant echo returned to haunt Robert two years later. After having to arrange for the untimely burial of his brother and sister-in-law, Robert received a letter from executor de Peyster in March of 1842 asking him to repay the balance of his $1,000 loan to Gordon. Evidently either uncle Phil Kearny's word of honour was as worthless as his nephew's, or executor de Peyster was reluctant to press Kearny on the subject of that surety, or worse.

In any case, Robert's response below seems as curt as the conventional language of the time would allow and leaves little doubt of his strong suspicion that the executors had cheated their British relatives and caused his brother's death.

(To Frederick de Peyster)

29 March 1842

My dear Sir,
I have received your letter of the 18th instant and beg to apprise you that the subject of its content had not escaped my recollection but I am waiting for a reply to my letter to you in January last for I feel indisposed to pay you money on account of my late brother's estate until I have first ascertained whether you paid him the full amount of the late John Watts legacy.

Robert N. Watts

No further letters appear in the available records from executor de Peyster. Wannabe financier P.J. Kearny died young, at the age of 36, and was buried in the family cemetery in Saugerties, NY in 1841. A letter from de Peyster to Robert indicated P.J. had died suddenly from an acute "constipation of the bowels." Apparently it was not deemed a homicide.

Charles Watts, having returned to England after his fruitless stay in New York, finally ended up appealing to brother Robert back in Canada for help in dealing with these smooth-tongued executors, who seem to have simply refused to pay him. Robert sued them. It was far too late to help poor Gordon, but it was not too late for Charles.

In early December 1845, estate executors Frederick De Peyster and P.J.'s uncle Phil Kearny, famous New York financier, were present in a New York court. On that day, following a court-supervised audit of their accounts and a review of John Watts' will, the judge ordered them to pay Charles the more than $3,000 owing to him from his uncle's estate, plus interest, and they were also to pay all costs of the audit and court costs.

In the grand scheme of things related to John Watts' fortune it seems a trivial amount of money. But Charles seems to have been less than successful himself — one source indicated he was deaf — and was apparently taking care of mother Sarah. The money certainly went a long way to make his and his wife's lives a bit more comfortable. Trivial in dollars or not, at the distance of a century and three-quarters it certainly seems to have been a non-trivial moral victory.

In the final letter of the series, in January 1846, Charles acknowledged Robert's help in resolving the issue, confirming that a note for the bequest had finally arrived. Ten years had elapsed, and two deaths.

But the sands of time quickly cover traumatic events, it seems, and by 1881 a well-regarded descendant of Frederick de Peyster was waxing lyrical in print about the de Peysters being in possession of what they called the Rose Hill estate.[33]

A year later, in April of 1847, Charlotte writes a cheery letter to her mother at Woodfield which mentions Sarah and her other children playing together in what seems to have been quite a loving and happy household,

"... The children have enjoyed this morning greatly and have just come in. I hear their little voices giving Sarah an account of a battle that Harriet had with the turkey cock, She seems to have come off victorious by her exulting tones – I suppose you would rather hear that she had concoured [sic] the alphabet that seems to be a very hard business however there are only a few letters now to learn. Laight brings her books every morning and her memory is so good that she learns with little trouble either to her self or me ...."

Several letters give more insight into Laight and her family's lives at Grantham Hall. Laight had a pony and was brought up "with lots of animals". Her father's stud farm seems to have been a lucrative occupation, at least for a time.

"The family went to the Carolinas each winter, driving there in a horse and buggy, I believe. It was in the Carolinas that the 'horse crowd' gathered in the cold weather."

Robert Nugent Watts was the first thoroughbred horse breeder in Canada, but the business went downhill when Watts lost his Scottish manager.

"Unfortunately, one day when they were walking around the grounds of Grantham Hall, [Robert] killed a snake. He picked it up with his cane, and threw it away. His aim was bad and the snake ended up coiled around the manager's neck. The manager was not amused. He quit and ... no more winters in horse country, southern U.S.A."

Notes indicate that when Robert was a Member of Parliament, the family spent at least some winters in Montreal.

"At that time it wasn't always safe to be an M.P. Once an angry mob chased [her father] into a butcher shop in Bonsecours Market and he had to hold them off with a butcher's knife. Parliament burned down and he helped carry out Queen Victoria's portrait for the 1st time. Someone else saved it from fire in Ottawa."

They didn't live there always, though, for Robert Nugent writes to his daughter Harriet an affectionate letter from Montreal, where that fiery Parliament of 1849 is sitting.

> *"My dear little Harriet*
> *This morning I have something to write which I think will be very entertaining to you and to your sisters because it is a true story and a very pretty one. – You will (I have no doubt) remember that I have often talked to you about two little girls Anna Maria and Henrietta, children of your aunt Susan who died in England some years ago. – Anna Maria died a few years ago at school leaving little Henrietta alone without having any sister to love or Mother to take care of her. – I used to call Henrietta, when she was no bigger that Willy [x] Tom sometimes and she used to kiss me and say dear Uncle do not call me Tom and I used to say No I won't my dear Tom and she answered, there you do it again dear Uncle. Laight will recollect all that and that dear little Tom had a sweet mild voice.*
> *Now I will tell you the rest of the story. – When little Henrietta grew big enough to leave school she went to Dublin to take care of her Papa who was there and five weeks past she married to Doctor Donald, who has brought her to Canada . . . . I did not know any thing about it but was invited to dine . . . and when I arrived there I looked very hard at the lady and asked her if I had not met her before . . . that I must have seen her somewhere when she was young and that my name was Watts. – She answered you must be my uncle Watts for whom I have letters in my box. – I wanted to take her to Drummondville to live with us and told her husband that he might come and see her sometimes. – but they both laughed and said they would come and see us and then go away together. Now is not that a pretty ending to the story about my dear Tom.*
> *God bless you my dear Child,*
> *Your affectionate Papa"*

Ten days before, he had written to Charlotte a vivid and entertainingly sardonic first-hand account of the burning of Montreal's Parliament building by a mob led by disgruntled Montreal Tories, who viewed the passage of the Rebellion Losses Bill as treasonous since it included amnesties and payments to French-Canadians. The second half of the letter is written in pencil.

> *"My dear Charlotte*
> *As the house was prorogued in rather a summary manner last evening by the Sovereign people, or rather by the loyal conservatives of Montreal, you will see me much sooner in all probability than either of us hoped for when I last wrote. Although the papers will contain many versions of the matter, as I was present and not an inattentive party to . . . events, the following description may be interesting.*
> *About 5 o'clock the Governor came down to the Legislative Council and assented to several bills; amongst them the Rebellion Losses Bill became law. On its being proclaimed by the clerk according to custom several lookers-on immediately left the strangers [visitors] gallery, with great stamping of feet. Anticipating some unusual proceeding out of doors a few of the members (amongst them myself) proceeded to see the Governor leave the buildings, in doing which he & his staff was helped and well pelted by eggs and apples of which good supply was at hand the market being close by . . . . We re-entered the building and were at work . . . between 8 and 9 in the evening when a few parties arrived breathless to say that a loyal meeting then being held on the Champ de Mars was moving to attack the Assembly . . . . A minute after the House was surrounded, the doors locked and stones flying in like hail. – You know how many windows there*

are to the House – on the first volley both auditors and Members sought such places of safety as seemed to offer the best protection and in less than five minutes I do not think there was a whole pane of glass – the members took refuge ... behind the speaker's chair. Wilson and myself happened to be the last .... presently, in rushed the rabble and upset the desks and chairs, ... when of a sudden the flames came rushing in ... we all rushed through the House, ran down stairs and finding the mob had left the door open, we escaped into the street (the mob having gone to the far end where the building was on fire) and retired unhurt. Finding the place clear and thinking it would continue so, I returned to the House to get my papers from my desk. The flames were then rushing into the body of the House and playing about the speaker's chair – some few minutes passed before I could find my desk but at last I got it and pocketed my papers and went into the street ... The pencil part is written from the Bonsecours Market ...

Your devoted husband,
RN Watts"

"Joseph Legaré, *The Burning of the Parliament Building in Montreal,* **about 1849. Courtesy Wikipedia"**

The bill had been meant to compensate for damages suffered during the Rebellion of 1837-38 in Lower Canada and represented vital social justice to French Canadians—proof also that responsible government could work for them. The Tories, however, saw it as a blatant rewarding of treasonous rebels.

The Reform-dominated legislature passed the bill over heated protests, but Tories still looked to the British-born governor to refuse his assent. Governor General Elgin did not: a responsible ministry with support of the parliamentary majority had recommended the measure. Ever the individualist, by the tone of Robert's letter, it seems that he was once again in conflict with his own local party members on the issue.

An appeal to Britain to disallow the bill by this group of Tories failed as well, and they then went on to agitate for annexation of the province to the United States. As was also to prove the case more than a century later, political unrest and violence led to Montréal's loss and Toronto's permanent gain. Canada's Parliament moved to Toronto and never returned to Quebec. In 1857 Queen Victoria named Ottawa as the capital.

Adopted Sarah died in 1859 at the age of 21 and was buried in the Watts family vault, a cemetery on the original Grantham Hall property, but which is now located between two fairways of the Drummondville Golf and Country Club.

Three years later, Robert and Charlotte's eldest daughter Laight Elizabeth Watts, Jean's great-grandmother, married an up-and-coming McGill University mathematician named Alexander Johnson.

Through 1866 Nugent, as his wife Charlotte called him, continued to be active "in the agricultural interest." He created and edited the Country Gazette Magazine, for which a year's subscription cost 3 shillings, nine pence, and he founded the Agricultural Society of Drummondville. He died in 1867.

That was a difficult year for the family, since Charlotte's father William also suddenly passed away that year. Robert was buried in the Watts vault mentioned above and Charlotte followed him in 1882, the year of their youngest daughter Margaret's wedding to Samuel Newton. She rests there together with her father (1867) and mother (1858).

"CHARLOTTE AND ROBERT NUGENT WATTS"

Generation Eight

Laight Elizabeth Watts and Alexander Johnson

(1840-1914)

On May 7th, 1862, Laight Elizabeth married eminent new Quebecker, Alexander Johnson, a 31-year-old protestant Irish graduate of Trinity College in Dublin, in a ceremony held in the country church of St. George's in Drummondville. This is a neo-Gothic stone building that had been built on land donated by her father less than ten years before. The church stands to this day, restored after being gutted by fire in 1863.

Johnson was a gold medalist graduate in mathematics and physics and had come to McGill in 1857 to become Professor of Mathematics and Natural Philosophy.

The Johnsons (no relation to the Johnson family that Polly Watts had married into) were an intellectual family, it seems, for Alexander's brother John also crossed the Atlantic to become Professor of Classics at Dalhousie University in 1863, and was to remain there for 31 years. John married Laight's sister, Harriet! The family must have been relatively well to do, to put two sons through Trinity. However, not much detail has come to light regarding their Belfast antecedents at the time of writing.

At McGill, Alexander obtained his M.A. in 1858 and LL.D in 1861. By 1867 he was Peter Redpath Professor of Pure Mathematics and Vice-Dean of the Faculty of Arts and eventually rose to Vice-Chancellor and Principal of the University before retiring in 1903 as Vice-Principal emeritus. He was appointed a Fellow of the Royal Society of Canada from the date of its founding by the Duke of Argyll in 1881, and Johnson became its President in 1905. He was quite a religious Anglican, was involved in the lay administration of the Church, and published a well-known textbook called, "Science and Religion" in 1876.

Family lore indicates that Johnson's opinions were strongly held and he was, perhaps, even something of a martinet. He detested Catholics – when son Alexander married a Catholic girl he was "promptly disowned." As a protestant Irishman hailing from Belfast in Ulster that was likely an inherited bigotry. Another handwritten anecdote from a granddaughter also describes a prejudice towards soldiers!

"Granny Johnson's wedding dress was altered to wear to dances and Alex. J., who was near-sighted, thought he saw his wife dancing with a military man and he went up to her and told her he had forbidden her to dance with the military. A strange woman replied, 'She was glad she wasn't his wife as this was her husband.'[!]"

Photographs do show a rather uncompromising set to Alexander Johnson's jaw, to go with his evidently very strong intellect and personality.

"Alexander Johnson"

Such a controlling sort of character was not out of step with the times, but strongly contrasted with what appears to have been Laight's own, rather more lighthearted personality. It also seems to have contrasted with his brother John's temperament, which seems to have had a bit more of a light touch, although he, too, seems to have been demanding of his students.

Doubtless, given the strength of her own lineage, Laight was able to cope with a perhaps domineering husband more than adequately. Her daughter wrote that *"He did have good points. My mother adored him."*

In any case, the Johnson household seems to have been run with less than rigid Victorian discipline, as there were no set times for the children to return for dinner. The eldest children, along with the household staff, looked after the younger ones. The couple entertained often in their elegant new home adjacent to the McGill University campus at 5 Prince of Wales Terrace.

"Alexander Johnson, Laight Johnson and daughter Elizabeth Laight, Feb. 1867"

This was the middle house of a prestigious and attractive row of nine limestone houses built in 1861 along the north side of Sherbrooke St. from the corner of McTavish Street. Several other people prominently associated with the university lived there as well.

Jean's mother wrote,

"Every Saturday the house was open for dances – he had a good wine cellar, small but exclusive. He was a friend of Sir John A. Macdonald. At formal dinners they would hire a butler, who was always told to watch how many glasses he gave to Sir John."

The family summered for years at Cap À L'Aigle, in the spectacularly beautiful Charlevoix region on the north shore of the St. Lawrence River east of Quebec City. This was near where the famous resort hotel le Manoir Richelieu was to be built in 1899, and at least two of the Johnson children were born there.

"Prince of Wales Terrace, courtesy McCord Museum, Montreal, file MP-1974.82"

It was there, also, that another chance meeting of relatives occurred. Richard deLancey Johnson was a younger brother of Sybil Johnson, from whom Jean is descended. Jean's mother related that the children were outside playing, when a carriage stopped and a woman excitedly rushed over. She had relatives named de Lancey and had overheard the name. She turned out to be the daughter of famous American novelist James Fenimore Cooper (The Last of the Mohicans), who had married Susan Augusta de Lancey. Later on, the Johnson family summered in England. It is unclear where they went, but family letters indicate that they did not have a lot of money, and spent time bicycling. Laight was not very good at it, and after a fall when she bruised one side of her face, she overheard a rude remark from an Englishwoman to the effect that, "I didn't know being a half-breed would be so obvious!"

Laight's photographic portrait, taken late in life, shows a charming little overbite, and hints strongly at latent good humour ready to bubble up at any time.

Laight Watts Johnson

Laight was evidently a charming and warm social being, making up for what her husband may have lacked in this aspect of his character. Newspaper obituaries describe her as the "Students' Friend",

"The late Mrs. Johnson was known to a very large circle of church and social workers throughout the city, and to the majority of the graduates of McGill during the time her husband was vice-principal . . . . they all entertained a sincere regard . . . a warm regard . . . for her. At Christmas time she used to invite to her home the students of all the faculties who had nowhere else to go."

Laight was also an active member of St. George's Church and a wide variety of other social agencies including the Ladies Auxiliary of McGill, the YMCA, the Dorcas Society, the Committee of the Church Home and a member of the Antiquarian Society. Her knowledge of the history of the family was called into use again when young son Alexander, born in 1868, brought home a stranger he had encountered in the street who was his double. This fellow turned out to be a descendant of Anne Watts, who had become Countess of Cassilis when she married Archibald Kennedy.

When John Johnson retired from Dalhousie in 1894, he and Harriet came to Drummondville, where she passed away in 1906. He died in 1914.[34] Laight Elizabeth Johnson also died in 1914, one year after her husband. Six daughters and three sons survived them, out of eleven.

Following her death, scholarly and adventurous son Guy Johnson established his physician offices in the house at Prince of Wales Terrace. Letters say that he looked too young to be accepted as a dollars a year, it seems likely that he had either imprudently borrowed that additional amount against the promised inheritance from some source in Quebec City, or used up the last of his bequest from his father, Stephen. Based on a legal document related to the wedding dowry of Stephen's sister in 1820, the largest portion of that inheritance had been in American interest-bearing paper, so perhaps it all went up the chimney in the same financial conflagration.

J.T.W. Hubbard, author of a history of the New York banking industry somewhat ironically entitled, "For Each, the Strength of All," quoted one contemporary investment banker thusly, "The immense fortunes which we heard so much about in the days of speculation have melted away . . . No man can calculate to escape ruin but he who owes no money."

And further, "Embezzlement by employees . . . played a major role in the collapse, as did bank officers lending to themselves or to close friends on insufficient collateral." Nearly a dozen banks failed in the month of May 1837.[30]

At the end of December 1837, P.J. writes to Gordon Watts a chatty letter cheerfully expounding his thoughts on the Rebellion of 1837, which had broken out the previous month in Lower Canada, and the attitudes of New Yorkers to that event. That appears to have been the last direct communication on paper from him to his creditors, apart from worthless promissory notes.[31]

By then he had lost all $17,000 of Gordon's money, worth nearly $350,000 today, and the reinvested interest on Charles' account as well.[32] In early 1838, Gordon became suspicious, wrote to P.J., received no reply, and sent his friend Macaulay to New York in an attempt to see what was going on, first hand. Doubtless Gordon, as a clerk in the military establishment, would have been unable to get free from work in the urgent days following the rebellion.

Macaulay, and Gordon and Robert's brother Charles, who had also travelled across the Atlantic from Jersey at the same time with similar concerns and intent, quickly got the picture. There is no evidence that Robert Nugent Watts was made aware of the precarious situation of his two brothers at that time. He likely also received an inheritance, but it appears he must have invested it without the assistance of P.J.

By June of 1838 the worst fears and suspicions of Macaulay and Charles Watts had been confirmed. They resolved, with de Peyster's apparent support, to try to get as much back as possible by simple persuasion, holding off on legal action supposedly to give P.J. a chance to find the money and pay up without having to go to court and face official ruin. After more than a month spent chasing P.J. around New York, Gordon's friend Macaulay, brother Charles, and de Peyster succeeded in nailing him down.

Although they estimated the chances of reselling the mortgage were nil because of the financial crisis, they did get some promises from P.J. on paper. Gordon was to get rent from the portion of the property he now owned, and regular interest on the mortgage. P.J. also pledged all his furniture to Gordon as part payment, but none of these liens were ever registered with the authorities.

Possibly as a result, little rent or interest ever seems to have materialized, and the other seven partners on the mortgaged house were strongly disinclined to either buy out P.J.s mortgage, or sell into a depressed market. Even the furniture pledge was voided, when the lot was seized without warning by the Sheriff's office in 1839. The Sheriff then had it auctioned off to satisfy some other creditor, recognized by the court but until then apparently unknown and unnamed. Gordon and Mary Watts, and their two-year-old daughter, Sarah, ended up with nothing but empty paper promises from P.J., executor de Peyster, and Kearny's famous 'Uncle Phil.'

Gordon and Charles were now in the entirely unenviable position of having to sue the Sheriff of a foreign country to get even the piddling sum of $1500 from the sale of the furniture. Perhaps out of pity, executor de Peyster advanced Gordon $1000 against P.J.'s promises to pay his debt. Not to worry physician when he graduated from McGill, so he had practiced medicine in a mining camp in Mexico, then at the Battle of Gallipoli with the Army, and after the war at London's famous Guy's Hospital following post-graduate work in Edinburgh.

But as the imposing housing development aged it also began to diminish. The houses nearest McTavish Street were purchased and replaced by a hotel, and the remaining buildings were bought by McGill, and subsequently demolished in 1971 to make way for the present Samuel Bronfman Building.

Laight's daughter Sybil, born on November 23, 1876, was to return to the Watts' home at Grantham Hall in Drummondville, for she married cousin Samuel Robert Newton, M. Sc., yet another McGill grad. Robert was the son of Sybil's Aunt Margaret, Laight's sister, who had inherited the Watts family estate and lived there with her husband Samuel Newton.

"Laight Watts Johnson and daughter Sybil"

Generation Nine

Sybil Watts and S. Robert Newton

(1876-1968)

Upon the death of their mother, Charlotte, in 1882, Grantham Hall appears to have passed to Laight's sister, Margaret. She loved horses, like her father, and also proved to be pretty canny at getting her own way. Tiny, she had been considered to be a sickly child, and apparently was not expected to survive childhood, although she had begun to ride horses at the age of two! Margaret quickly learned that if she complained of a headache she would be allowed to skip her studies and go out for some fresh air.

She would then go riding, and she became a 'fantastic' horsewoman. Although she stood only about five feet, two inches tall, she was strong and she lived until the ripe old age of 84, still driving horses until a few days before she died. Her granddaughter related that she was still ramrod straight and beautiful, too, at that age. Margaret played piano beautifully and showed her horses at Toronto's Royal Winter Fair, where she sold one particular horse that apparently loved the show ring, but was otherwise badly behaved.

"Margaret Newton (driving)"

As the story goes, this horse was a champion that year at the Royal and an American gentleman offered to buy him. He asked the price and then asked petite Margaret if the apparently flawless horse had any faults. Her honest, if brief, answer was, "Yes, he kicks." The potential customer then wanted to know who usually drove him, and Margaret told him she always did, leaving out the extra but completely unnecessary fact that her husband could not handle the animal and that she invariably drove the horse from the back seat of a four-seated buggy to avoid hooves regularly flying up near her face!

The American gentleman bought the horse and seeing Margaret the next day made a point of telling her, "You told me he kicked, and he does!" Granddaughter Alexandra remembered having fun driving with her in a sleigh in winter and a buggy in the summer.

The year her mother died, Margaret married Samuel Newton. The Newton family has documented history back into ancient times, but which branch Samuel is descended from is obscure. He seems to have been listed in the 1851 British census at the age of two as a "lodger" in the Newton household in Manchester, England. Perhaps his mother and father had perished.

"Samuel Newton"

Margaret and Samuel Newton's son, Robert, married Laight's daughter, Sybil, Jean's grandmother, in 1909. Sybil married late for the times, at the age of 33, and her wedding to Samuel Robert (Bob) Newton took place in St. George's Church in Montreal on October 8, 1909. A silver-embossed wedding invitation survives, tied with a silk ribbon.

"Front Row, left to right: Miss Smith, Helena Johnson, Sybil Johnson (bride), Jill Johnson, Nennie Budden. Back Row, left to right: John Poyart, unidentified, Stephen Newton, Robert Newton (bridegroom), Elizabeth Johnstone, Dr. DeLancey Johnson"

***"From left to right, Charlotte (Watts) McDougall (sister of Laight), Sybil
(Johnson) Newton, Margaret (Watts) Newton, possibly Ella Newton"***

Jean's mother, Alexandra was the daughter of Samuel Robert Newton and Sybil Johnson. Alexandra describes Sybil as having been home schooled, supplemented by a course in French at McGill. Sybil was a gregarious woman, but she was a teetotaler and she taught the children from one of her mother's social agencies not to drink – ever. She loved golf and curling.

The happy couple settled in nearby Sherbrooke, where they raised two daughters, Alexandra and her sister, Margaret. Sybil was a long-time member of St. Peter's Church there. Her husband, S. Robert (Bob) Newton, was born in Drummondville, no doubt at Grantham Hall, in 1882, and attended school locally at Dufferin Grammar School in Brigham before attending McGill. He graduated with an engineering degree in 1902 and began working for Canadian Ingersoll-Rand the following year. He rose to become vice-president of the company during his 41 years there. He was also a director of the Brompton Pulp Co. and Vice-President of the Newton Construction Company, which he founded with his brother Stephen G. Newton. The two of them were honoured by having Rue Newton named for them in the old north district of the city of Sherbrooke.

Robert was always very sports-minded, and an excellent athlete. He played on school hockey and baseball teams and he became a highly skilled marksman. Two medals have been preserved which commemorate his ability, one from the Grand Trunk Riverside Gun Club dated March 4, 1922 and a second won at the British Empire Exhibition of 1924 at Wembley. Robert also travelled to the 1924 Paris Olympic Games as a member of the Canadian trapshooting team, which tied the Finns for the silver medal in the event. The United States won gold. In the individual competitions, Bob was second only to a man named Cooey, from Toronto.

Hubert Joseph Cooey was the founder and owner of H. W. Cooey, a renowned machine shop and arms manufacturer in Cobourg, Ontario, later purchased by Winchester. Cooey's .22-caliber rifle won a certificate of honour at Wembley that year. It, and the company's 12-gauge Model 84 shotgun are Canadian collector's items today.[35][36]

Robert was a city councilor in Sherbrooke from 1921 to 1930 and chaired the committee of gas and electricity and also the parks committee. From 1936 he was in a leadership position on the Board of Bishop's University and from 1943-44 he was vice-president of the executive committee. He also served as treasurer and president of the executive committee of an exclusive girl's boarding school, King's Hall, in nearby Compton, Quebec, remaining on the Board for twenty-two years. Two $500 annual bursaries were established in his honour after he died in 1944.[37] [38] [39]

Both Samuel and Margaret were buried in the Watts family cemetery now located in the middle of the Drummondville Golf Club. As late as 1985 there remained Newtons in Sherbrooke and the cemetery was still being maintained.

"Above: Robert Newton (second from right, back row) and the Canadian Olympic trapshooting team, 1924. Below: Robert and Sybil en route to Paris."

"Silver Medal Award. Note Baron de Coubertin's signature at bottom right."

In the early twentieth century, Grantham Hall was sold to a family named Marler, and was destroyed by fire in 1922.

Alexandra married Bert Millward, on June 20, 1936, and their daughter, Jean, who represents the eleventh generation, commissioned this story. At this point we leave off the narrative — but not before revealing a few details about the courtship of Alexandra and Bert! During the Great Depression of the 1930s cash was very scarce and their entertainment was restricted to a few dances, although all the great bands of the day played at tea dances in Montreal, which made them very exciting. Alexandra related that most of her dates with Bert consisted of going to a restaurant and drinking coffee at five cents a cup. Bert graduated in 1934 and taught at St. Andrew's College, a boys' boarding school in Aurora, Ontario, north of Toronto, which continues to thrive to this day. By interesting coincidence, the author was a student there during the mid-1960s, and his sister attended King's Hall during that time as well.

Appendix: Watt

According to one source, the founder of the English branch of the family Watt was one Sir Michael le Fleming, a Knight from Flanders, who arrived in Britain leading some forces under William the Conqueror in 1066, sent by Baldwin V, Earl of Flanders. He would have been assigned to William's right wing at the Battle of Hastings. Sir Michael must have been a true and well-trusted warrior, for some years later, King William assigned him a daunting task — opposing the Scots on the northern borders of his domain.

Defending Brittania from the northerners had forced the Romans to build Hadrian's Wall, nearly a thousand years before. But Gaelic warriors were not his only problem. William had so difficult a time with rebellious Anglo-Saxons that he marred his reign with what became known as the Harrying of the North in 1069-70. It is unknown whether Sir Michael was involved with this campaign, which involved burning villages, slaughtering the inhabitants and salting the earth. One chronicler records, probably rhetorically, that more than 100,000 of the Anglo-Saxon inhabitants perished. Survivors resorted to cannibalism. In 1086 the Domesday returns still record the status of many estates "wasteas est" (it is wasted). On his deathbed, William regretted his cruelty in the north . . ."I am stained with the rivers of blood that I have shed." It is not recorded what Sir Michael felt about it.

In any case, Sir Michael performed his duties to the satisfaction of his Lord, for he, like other officers in William's army, was awarded large (formerly Saxon and Danish) landholdings, castles and manors in Lancashire, along with the castles and the lordship of Beckermet and estates in Cumberland. A branch of the le Flemings settled in a place called Wath in Yorkshire, which was at the epicenter of the Harrying, as Lords of Wath. It is entirely possible that one of the sons of the Lords of Wath eventually made his way north to serve David I, King of Scotland, who is known to have been affiliated with the Norman descendants of William and to have brought a number of their concepts of government to the north. As mentioned earlier in this story, one Watts family legend has it that John Watt of Edinburgh had a charter going back to King David.

It continued to be a bloody time, especially in Yorkshire, but most everywhere in Europe as well. By the late 1300s, the Lords of Wath were becoming Wathes, and Sir Thomas Wathes of Eston served under Henry V in the French Wars, possibly at Agincourt, and was granted estates along the Loire around 1420 as reward for his loyal service there.

His grandson, Sir Richard Wattys, fought under the white rose banner of the York faction of the royal House of Plantagenet against the red rose army of Lancaster, and fell at the battle of Wakefield in 1460 with his master, Richard, Duke of York. A year later, the Yorkists prevailed, ending the Wars of the Roses, and the Tudor dynasty began.

By 1511, the name of John Wattes first appears. Elizabeth I awards him estates confiscated from the Knights Hospitallers of St. John of Jerusalem in 1560 during the dissolution of the Catholic Monasteries of England, which was begun by her father Henry VIII. The Wattes continue to be very highly regarded by the Crown, and continue to increase their wealth, for John's grandson, William Watts, married Mary Montagu, whose grandmother was the daughter of King Edward I. Their descendants are "founders kin" to All Souls's College, Oxford, and part of this royal bloodline. William died in 1614.

But the English Civil War, culminating in the execution of Charles I in 1642, seems to have cast a shadow over the family, who for the first time chose the wrong side, fighting for the Royalists against Cromwell. The family's huge British estates began to vanish. The victorious Parliamentarians confiscated some. Some were given away to strangers. Some were lost in the South Sea stock market investment Bubble in the next century.

There is at present no documentary evidence that the Watt family of Edinburgh, which one can safely assume went back decades before 1596 in that location, are related directly to the Le Fleming family whose story is sketched in bare bones in this Appendix. No records appear to exist at the present time which might say yea or nay. But it is entirely possible. Le Flemings settled next to the border, and the name Wattes appears there at roughly the same time we have Wat, and Watt, and Watts appearing a couple of hundred miles away to the north, in Scotland.

Did one of those Waths, Wattys, or Wattes, possibly a second or third son, barred from inheriting, make his way to the north? Another researcher will have to discover the answer.

Bibliography

(Endnotes)

1   Robert Chambers, DOMESTIC ANNALS OF SCOTLAND, W. & R. Chambers, Edinburgh, 1858, Vol. 1, p. 348.

2   Albert Welles, Watts (Watt) In New York and Edinburgh, Scotland. Charles H. Ludwig, New York, 1898, p. 27

3   D.A.Story, THE DELANCEYS: A ROMANCE OF A GREAT FAMILY, Thomas Nelson & Sons Ltd., Canada, 1931.

4   New York Gazette, or Weekly Post-Boy, October 23, 1752. Copyright NewsBank and/or the American Antiquarian Society, 2004.

5   J.W. de Peyster, LOCAL MEMORIALS RELATING TO THE DE PEYSTER AND WATTS AND AFFILIATED FAMILIES, Charles H. Ludwig, New York, 1881,p.49

6   Welles, p. 3.

7   http://www.maybole.org/history/articles/kennedy/portraits.htm

8   Welles, p.13

9   New York Gazette, or Weekly Post-Boy, December 17, 1770. Copyright NewsBank and/or the American Antiquarian Society, 2004.

10   Earl Thomas, Sir John Johnson, Loyalist Baronet. Dundurn Press, Toronto, 1986, p.61

11   The Papers of Sir William Johnson, University of the State of New York, Albany, NY 1921-1965, v. 7, p. 1144

12   Thomas, p. 71

13   Welles, p. 5.

14   J.W. de Peyster, p.49.

15   http://www.middlesex-heraldry.org.uk/publications/monographs/mdxchurches/mdxchurches-stolavehartst.htm

16   http://royalyorkers.ca/lights/lc_cp_watts.htm

17   Gavin K. Watt. POISONED BY LIES AND HYPOCRISY, Dundurn Press, Toronto, 2014, p. 24, Ch. 8.

18   British Library. Sloane and Additional Manuscripts, Add MSS 21722, Register of Letters to Various Persons, 1778; National Archives of Canada, Haldimand Collection, microfilm reel number A-663.

19   http://www.herriottheritage.org/pdf/scotland.pdf

20   https://www.igenea.com/en/surname-projects/h/herriott-1710

21   The Canadian Antiquarian and Numismatic Journal, Series 3, Vol VIII, No. 2, p. 53. C. H. Marchand, Montreal, 1911.

22   Personal communication from Les de Belin, lesdebelin@bigpond.com 2013

23   Les de Belin, lesdebelin@bigpond.com 2013.

24   Antiquarian Journal, p. 61.

25   http://www.biographi.ca/en/bio/heriot_frederick_george_7E.html

26   Margery Durham Campbell. A LONG LIFE. Andrew Reid & Company, Ltd. Newcastle-Upon-Tyne, 1925, p.22.

27   http://www.biographi.ca/en/bio/sheppard_william_9E.html

28   http://www.biographi.ca/en/bio.php?id_nbr=3814&print=1

29   http://www.biographi.ca/en/bio.php?id_nbr=3790

30   J.T.W. Hubbard, FOR EACH, THE STRENGTH OF ALL: A HISTORY OF BANKING IN THE STATE OF NEW YORK, New York University Press, New York 1995, p. 92-93.

31   Letter from P.J. Kearney to Gordon, 30th December, 1837

32   http://mykindred.com/cloud/TX/Documents/dollar/index.php?cyear=1836

33   de Peyster

34   P.B. Waite, The Lives of Dalhousie University, V. 1, 1818-1925. McGill-Queen's University Press, Montreal & Kingston, 1994.

35   Sherbrooke Daily Record, July 28, 1924.

36   http://progress-is-fine.blogspot.ca/2013/04/we-used-to-make-things-in-this-country_16.html

37   La Nouvelle de Sherbrooke, 2 au 9 Janvier, 1993, p. 9

38   La ville électrique. Sherbrooke, 1880-1988. Les editions Olivier, Sherbrooke, QC, 1988.

39   Personal letter from Board of King's Hall, Compton.

Printed in the United States
By Bookmasters